The Art and Craft of
Classical Guitars

100th Anniversary Edition

by Manuel Rodríguez

HAL•LEONARD®

Updated 100th Anniversary Edition
Copyright © 2003, 2009 by Manuel Rodríguez

Published in 2009 by Hal Leonard Books
An Imprint of Hal Leonard Corporation
7777 West Bluemound Road
Milwaukee, WI 53213

Trade Book Division Editorial Offices
19 West 21st Street, New York, NY 10010

Printed in the United States of America

Library of Congress Cataloging-in-Publication Data is available upon request.
ISBN 978-1-4234-8035-8

www.halleonard.com

Dedication

With my most sincere affection:

To my wife Emilia, my life companion, and a collaborator in my work.

To my mother, for her dedication to us.

To my father, my best master and friend.

To my son, Norman, my craftsman, and my son Manuel, my entrepreneur, his wife Elen and my beloved grandson Manuel IV.

To our friend and brother Arthur E. Macbeth, who in these last forty years has done so much good for the Rodríguez family. Thank you, Arthur.

To my friends Maja and Santiago Tovar who, together with Mr Kumentat, made the German edition of this book possible.

To Real Musical, its directors and collaborators, who made the Spanish edition of this book possible.

To Mr. Maurice J. Summerfield and Mr. Colin Cooper for this English edition.

And on behalf of the Rodríguez family and their collaborators in the construction of our guitars:

To our representatives in the USA, UK and the rest of world and their salesmen.

To the music stores, for making it possible for our friends the guitarists to enjoy our guitars.

Many thanks to you all.

Manuel Rodríguez

AUTHOR'S NOTE

Simply a Guitar Luthier

As the reader of this book will soon realize, I am not really a writer. I am a guitar luthier, and I am neither good nor bad at that.

The Rodríguez family has decided that the proceeds from the sale of this book be given to charitable organizations to be chosen in the future. I confess, dear reader, that I have no pretension of teaching anyone anything or showing them how to make a guitar, let alone of displaying my expertise to those who know more than I do. My intention in all this is that the ordinary guitarist who purchases a guitar, whether it is their first musical instrument or whether they wish to acquire a new and better one, should obtain some historical, human, and basic technical knowledge of the instrument they have chosen with which to express themselves.

The history of the guitar in the world has many stages and gaps as far as its development goes. My hope is that this book will take you as close as possible to the trajectory of this stringed instrument, from its very beginnings to the creation of the guitar that you play today.

Numerous are those of us who have gone into the business of making such a beautiful human-shaped box, made from precious woods, which are beautiful and unique in their growth, as compared to the rest of the arboreal species.

The luthier guitar-making craftsman, throughout the ages, has experienced prolonged economic hardships and has not known very many bonanzas. This is why no guitar luthier, at the end of his days, left any large fortune. He simply lived and felt the enthusiasm and the great pleasure of making a musical instrument of some likeness to his being, thanks to his trade, technique, and art. Making guitars and satisfying the desires of the person who plays music with the guitar that one has created is the only objective. Today, it is a different world altogether.

From the end of the World War II in the mid-1940s to the years after that, the world became prosperous and people felt an appetite for new cultural horizons—among which the door of curiosity opens to our guitar. Eminent concert guitarists, headed by Maestro Andrés Segovia, aroused great enthusiasm in the whole world with their performances. There was a proliferation of trained teachers who enriched the teaching of our guitar in every corner of the planet.

In the 1960s, the world needed classical and flamenco guitars, and there was a high demand for them. Capital was mobilized and one had a whole range to choose from. But in such proliferation—mass production for that matter—there have always been "know-it-alls" who proclaim themselves experts in guitar making, just as such "experts" arise in other sectors in this dear world of ours. Star guitar makers of the day are born, pens write what they are told by others who in turn have heard from someone else. To my way of thinking, this is quite excusable, a direct result of humanizing our instrument.

We have a saying, which goes: "Man puts his hope in man." What I am writing in these pages is mainly my own personal experiences, and the rest is borne out of my research in these last five years when I decided to put everything into writing.

So, kind reader, I would therefore ask you to overlook my errors (and my space saving convention of using the personal pronoun "he" instead of the lengthier—albeit more politically correct—"he or she" and their corresponding case forms; I wish that no offense be taken by the many fine and talented female luthiers and other artists implied in this convention), and honor the points I get right.

Manuel Rodríguez, Sr.

Contents

Dear
Bill

Thank you for ...

... ...

... ...

Best

[signature]

Chapter 1

The Guitar: Musical and Artistic Instrument.
Its Art and Development.

*La guitarra
hace llorar a los sueños.
El sollozo de las almas
perdidas,
se escapa por su boca
redonda.
Y como la tarántula
teje una gran estrella
para cazar suspiros,
que flotan en su negro
aljibe de madera.*

FEDERICO GARCÍA LORCA

A musical instrument is, without doubt, one of the most ingenious inventions of man. Take the violin, for example. What a marvellous and flawless creation! There is nothing, with the exception of the scroll, that is ornamental in the violin. Everything—absolutely everything—in this instrument is conceived to perform a specific purpose. In spite of its functionality, we behold it as an instrument of extraordinary elegance. One cannot imagine all the thousand and one changes this instrument has undergone throughout the ages before it finally got to what it is now. Only the great masters of Cremona—Stradivari and Guarneri—were able to create, thanks to their common sense, logical minds, and much inspiration, this unsurpassable work of art. At every stage of history, luthiers have striven and endeavoured, through their creativeness, to construct a beautifully sounding instrument that gives satisfaction to the ears and whose shape is a delight to the eyes. Nothing evokes sound as vividly as its outward design and appearance; and this precisely explains why an instrument made to produce music is an art piece.

Guitar making is therefore more of an art than craftsmanship. An explanation is needed here. Experts hold the theory that what really makes art is the fact that the artistic object is unrepeatable. Well, a guitar can never be repeated. No guitar sounds exactly the same as another, no matter how hard its maker tries to make it do so. This is because a lot of factors intervene in its creation: from the choice of wood and its use in making any given guitar, which may be number X of your production, to thinking of the end user, a particular guitarist, a country, the season of the year, and the atmospheric conditions under which the instrument is created; even the maker's own moods, have a bearing on the guitar.

In the 1960s, together with my friends in Los Angeles (USA), we came up with a plan to seek grants from the Ford Foundation to, through research, develop the guitar scientifically. We consulted with a group of eminent engineers who, well-versed in acoustics, had helped in the designing of the Los Angeles Music Centre. After a series of talks and explanations to familiarize them with the main features of guitar construction, they came to the conclusion that the construction of this instrument involves many *imponderable* (that which cannot be weighed, measured, or determined with precision; defying any forecast) aspects.

Once you get the wood, you have to remember that each piece, even though it may come from the same board and the same cut, is different—different as to its homogeneity with the whole piece, as to the measurement of the bracings, cross bars; in short, different as to its soundboard. Drawing an analogy with human beings, we could well say that though daughters of the same mother, every sister is different. Likewise, every guitar, even though coming from the same wood, is different in its interior construction. The end result is therefore unpredictable, seeing that one of the unforeseeable factors is the construction process itself.

Another aspect, which defies any forecast in each guitar, is the pressure of the sides and the effect of gluing them to the soundboard. This technique is pure and simple. It is a skill acquired from long experience and devotion, with the result that every guitar, made from high-quality woods, plus the experience of a great luthier and the highest instinct and dignity, is different. Thus, if that which cannot be repeated is art, then, my respectable colleagues, in my modest view, our guitar is also an artistic instrument. It is even more so if each artist constructs his guitar by working an exclusive ornament, on the precious and unique woods, a mosaic which distinguishes the soundhole from all the soundholes of his or her other guitars (Torres never made the same soundhole design twice). It is like a feather, a purfling that will never be repeated as far as color, thickness and taste are concerned. We are therefore talking about an art piece that has a life of its own, produces sound, and provides the guitarist with his own instrument to express his musical skill and harmonic knowledge, held in the hands and close to the body; an art piece or pieces of precious woods put together to the luthier's taste and woodworking skills; your trade, personality, and dignity in doing a good job. The guitarist plays the guitar, which is either a top-quality musical instrument or an art piece, which the guitar maker can never repeat.

The artistic luthier, who in the past constructed guitars with great artistic skill, but today neglects innovation or has simply lost the skill, will find it quite impossible to make a value judgement, or to feel that the instrument constructed on their premises is an art piece—this in spite of their knowledge of pictorial art and their awareness that duplication is common.

Whereas the former creates a musical instrument of art, the latter makes duplicate instruments from an archetype called a guitar. Although, in all fairness, it must be said that never in the history of guitar lutherie have guitars been reproduced with such high quality. The guitar that is mass-produced (that is, the guitar as an object) can—thanks to smart and special tools, a good choice of wood, and proper drying process—currently meet quality standards and provide musicians with a perfect instrument as far as price, presentation, sound quality, and user-friendliness are concerned. Until now, such has been quite unthinkable. This really makes it easier for any guitarist to lay hands on a fitting instrument that suits their taste and falls within their musical requirements, performance needs and economic range. And in some cases, the guitar falls within the range of good quality and good wood construction.

The luthier—not the manufacturer of objects—manages to make an instrument that produces an attractive sound, has a fantastic outward appearance and is faithful to the handcrafted guitar. The luthier—that is, the artist of a renowned musical tradition who makes an instrument, thanks to long experience acquired in years of practice—is obliged to turn the instrument that he constructs into an unrepeatable art piece. The woods used in its creation must be unique, and with them the luthier must create a unique ornamental design for the guitar in question. With these exclusive woods he must manage to produce an instrument of sustainable, top-quality sound, an equilibrium in tone through the fingerboard, treble, and powerful singing. Moreover, he must make this instrument easy to play and craft it so as to provide everything the guitarist expects from a guitar.

Given this opportunity, the luthier is called upon to create for posterity an instrument that will serve as living proof of his creative skills in the trade of woodcraft. For instance, I have right before my eyes this magnificent book *Musical Instruments* by A. Brüchner. We can observe in its pages a 16th-century soprano lute with marvellous bone incrustation and marquetry on the top, body, neck, fingerboard, and headstock. To be sure, the luthier who created it believed he was creating an art piece, and possibly even more so did the person who was to own it, G. Sellas (Venice, 1750). What wonderful incrustations on the soundhole, purfling, fingerboard, headstock! What a delightful sight if you stop a moment to take a look at the filigree on the back, side, and the neck! These instruments were very impressive for their epoch, and it was delightful to listen to their music. The player needed the same things that today's guitarist needs: clear sound, power in all the registers, harmony, and tuning. In short, they needed and used their musical instruments. And more than that, they turned them into works of art whose ornamentation, delicacy, and design are a delight for us today. Harp makers worked in a similar fashion. Even today, art harps are still being created; and the violin luthier is always on the lookout for the beauty of line, incrustations, and wood of the violin, viola, and violoncello. The satisfaction of a perfect design harmony of the instrument delights the violinist's sight and taste.

If art is man's capacity to create beauty, then there should be no doubt in anybody's mind that musical instruments, in general, and the guitar, in particular, are beautiful.

In Europe, during the 16th and 17th centuries, magnificent guitars were made. And with the opportunity provided through the construction of this musical instrument, pure art was at work in its carving, headstock, excroups, bridges, and buttons; not to mention the marquetry, mother-of-pearl incrustations, ivory, and ebony woods and other precious materials. Well, they took great pleasure in their love for the instrument.

1.1. The Guitar: Stringed Musical Instrument. Its Birth.

As we have already said, many are the imponderables of this music-making instrument. Just the wood alone—the most important ingredient of all—accumulates a whole series of complexities in its density, hardness, and elasticity. Without any doubt, the guitar that we luthiers build is the instrument with the most pieces of all stringed instruments (for personally, I do not consider the piano to be a stringed instrument, but rather one that has strings).

Let us retrace its origin, shall we? Man, out of need for subsistence, invented the bow and arrow as an indispensable hunting weapon. This was possibly how the first stringed instrument came into being, as a sound was surely made as the bow was pulled to shoot the arrow. A similar thing must have happened with the seashell as a string slid over it. This discovery was, certainly, the appreciation by humans that by skilful handling they could create so many different resonances: from a string stretched by a cane, to canes forming all kinds of squarish shapes that held several strings, to a turtle shell and strings. So this was how, thanks to the imagination and creativity that man started developing, sound- and noise-making objects were born. The Samarian Lute (2400 BC), the Indian Ravawastron (1000 BC), the Turkestan Capuz (500 BC), the Chinese Tuen-Kin (300 BC), or the moon-shaped guitar are some of their precursors. The whole of mankind had the same curiosity.

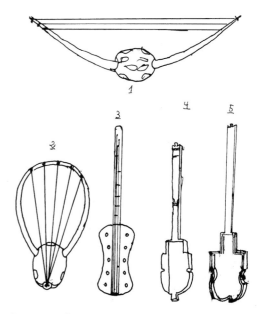

Ancestors of our stringed instruments:
1) Prototype of a theoretical harp, with tortise shell soundboard.
2) Idea of a lyre with a shell soundboard.
3) Long-necked instruments from the Hittite Kingdom, 1900 years before the Christian era. Possibly the first idea of a guitar shape.
4 & 5) Other guitar shapes found in Egypt at the Coptic monastery.

To reach the human ideal of sound production became an objective that injected more impetus in its development. What began as the production of noises and rudimentary sounds evolved to incorporate volume and other sound features.

However, their different designs and appearances are also noteworthy. The lyre, made from an animal shell, or the instrument created from half an earthenware pot, on whose circumference two circular horn-shaped sticks rest (the five strings making up the set end up together at the back of the pot), are some examples. It is also worth mentioning the Egyptian Turkestan Dutar (300 BC), a sort of instrument with a long neck, a string, and its corresponding button. The string is stretched over a round body with a flat top—possibly made of animal skin—that ends up at the back of the box.

All these instruments flourished; and throughout the Mediterranean, music was created with them. In oriental countries, even today, people are still composing with these instruments or others derived from them.

What magnificent literature and historical and artistic information we possess on the curiosity, creativity, and in many cases, the instinctive yearning of the human being to make instruments that produce music.

As history unfolded and time went by, an infinity of stringed objects were created, through whose melodies people expressed their joys and sorrows. The sole aim of these early instruments was to create the best sound-producing object possible. The Ravanastron (1000 BC, India) the different kinds of lute (1400–300 BC), or the tanbur from the Egyptian civilization (prodigious in stringed instruments) are just a few of the most prolific examples of the human interest in, and invention of, beautiful instruments with which to express feelings.

The first idea of what was to become the guitar of our days can be traced back to the Coptic lute. This instrument, found in a Coptic monastery in Egypt in 300 AD, consists of a long neck fixed to a square box on the upper part. As it got to the middle of the piece it formed a belt, which rounded the lower part.

13th Century Spanish Guitars
The guitarra morisca and the guitarra latina from the Cántigas de Santa Maria de Alfonso el Sabio.

However, it was in the confluence between Asia and Europe that the various versions of lutes thrived: the Mizhar-Barbat, the rebab, and the oud. Aesthetically, their shapes were that of a pear; a peculiarity that served to identify stringed instruments among the Arab, Asian, and European peoples.

This same shape characterized our lute, banduria, and mandolin which, together with the guitar, gave rise to the flourishing of the numerous groups of serenaders or pluck and plectrum instrument groups—a natural name for these musical groups.

Originating from villages and little towns, these groups were mainly formed by self-taught musicians who generated the pop and folk music that form part of the musical culture of Spain today.

Getting back to the Spanish historical and musical past, we must put a special emphasis on the Arab domination from North Africa. After winning the battle of Jerez in 711 AD, they settled with their culture and developed it in Spain for a lengthy period of time. Already in the 8th and 9th centuries, various forms of the lute were in use.

Hence the importance of the "Cantigas de Santa María" (medieval poems set to music) by Alfonso X the Wise, preserved in the El Escorial Monastery library (Madrid). In these marvellous and richly decorated pages you can find reproductions of drawings of the different forms of stringed musical instruments that existed in Spain between 1257 and 1275. From the vignettes we can see how they are played with the fingers, as well as with a bow. From these works of art we are given insight into the great discovery—possibly scientific—of these types of instruments; precursors of the present day ones, and the fruit of the intuition and imagination of someone with unbounded eagerness for getting more sound from a string. What this someone could never have imagined was the grandeur of the bow, which gave rise to the instruments of the violin family, and paved the way for the fantastic luthier craftsmen—the same craftsmen who, in the medieval period, created violins that have never been surpassed. They used only two kinds of wood: the pine and the maple, which, upon scientific analysis of today, turn out to be the two woods that best transmit vibrations.

If we consider the nature and transmission of sound, and compare the average speed and the meters reached per second, we obtain the following table:

Western red cedar	4,400 m/s
Spruce	4,790 m/s
Maple	4,000 m/s
Water	1,437 m/s
Steel	5,000 m/s
Aluminum	6,420 m/s
Glass	5,500 m/s
Cork	480 m/s

What can we say about the use of such specific and unique woods in the construction of these instruments? A scientific discovery or a luthier's intuition?

If intuition is the intellectual act that garners knowledge about things through perception alone without reasoning, then you can draw your own conclusions.

Not only were these two types of wood used to create these wonderful stringed instruments, but they also made fine-tuning and harmonic perfection possible. The great human imagination only had to blend the greatness of these sounds with those of other instruments. Well, this then is a simple definition of what we today call an orchestra, the delight of mankind.

But the most evident thing of all is that, in the course of their construction, the exquisiteness of the sound of these music-making instruments produces the emotion of being and creating art. There are plenty of books illustrated with

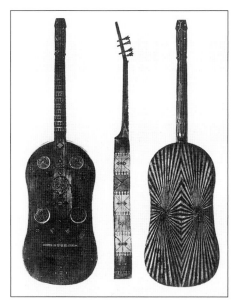

1•Vihuela, c. 1500, Spain
Musée Jacquemart-André, Paris.

images of the skill and art of those maestros who, in their eagerness for aesthetic improvement, the enhancement of the sound, and in their attempt to make them easy to play, were more concerned about this aspect. The reader should consider the baroque lutes, the harps, the violas, and the violins as proof of this fact.

A common feeling shared by every luthier, from medieval times until now, is how to obtain an instrument of great volume and quality sound. All the same, following the example of the maestros before us, it is also necessary to have the pleasure and the joy of creating in each one of our guitars the personality and style of the luthier: well-defined sounds, ease of playing, and distinctive decoration.

Just imagine, my kind and patient reader, the emotion and delicate satisfaction of creative joy that my illustrious colleague, José de Frías experienced as he created the Spanish guitar in Seville in 1777, with its ornamentation, mother-of-pearl top, soundhole and purfling, its marquetry on the back, sides, neck, and headstock, and its delicate buttons. And all that incrustation work by candlelight.

Likewise, my honorable colleague and compatriot, Lorenzo Alonso (Madrid, 1786), expressed his style in the incrustations of the soundhole, the top, the back and the sides. There is nothing more valuable to a luthier father than leaving his son his good workmanship, declaring his child, at the age of four, a professional guitar maker. This son would later on become a consummate violin maker (Maestro Sor mentions him in his method).

This is how we arrive at the so-called *modern guitar*, evaluated by some bright scientist who questioned the skill, sensitiveness, and professionalism of the former masters. Maestro Antonio Torres is confirmed to be the creator of the fan bracing system that reinforces the inside of the guitar top. Compared to instruments before then, Torres can be said to have been a visionary scientist.

It is a well-known fact that Torres did not go beyond elementary school and therefore must have had an education of equivalent level. What he must have been was a natural talent and an inveterate thinker who developed his thoughts with practical common sense. But nobody obtained—and Torres was possibly no exception—the illumination of his ideas through divine apparition, but rather from his attentiveness logical precedents, and his already-mentioned common sense that allowed him to come up with improvements in guitar construction. His repairing of other guitars enabled him to get ideas and thus boosted his subsequent work. According to the master guitarist and eminent pedagogue Dionisio Aguado, Juan Moreno (1792–1836), a guitar maker from Madrid, reinvented guitar construction. He superimposed the fingerboard on the top and put fan bracing inside the soundboard.

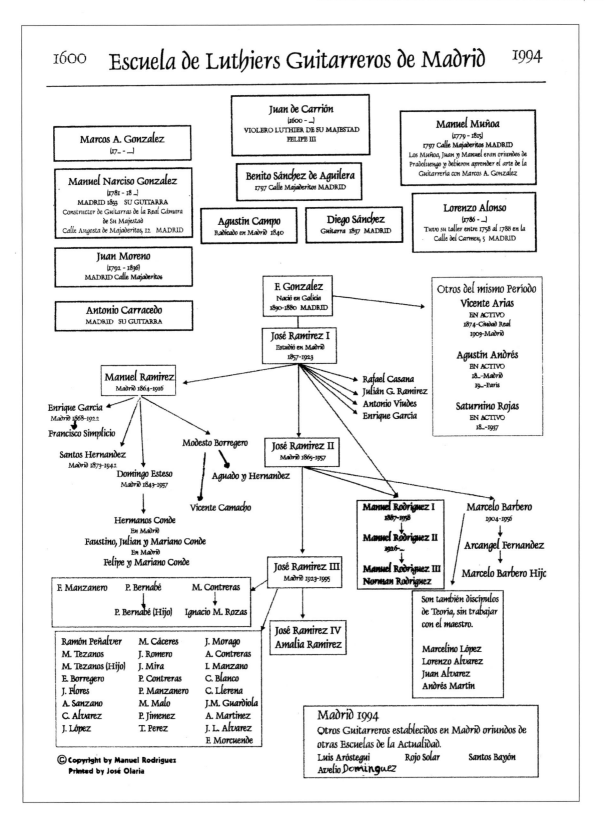

Antonio Torres

Antonio Torres was born in Almería in June 1817. Nobody can say for certain whether, since they lived far apart, Torres could have laid hands on a guitar by Juan Moreno (1792–1836) that needed repairing. What is also not known is whether Torres, in his first guitars, had already constructed them with the fingerboard superimposed on the soundboard, or whether he had created some of them with the frets on the soundboard and the fingerboard level with the soundboard. Or perhaps he had access to knowledge on guitar construction.

The guitar was, during Torres's time, already being made with the fingerboard over the top. It is not known whether the master made any guitars with the frets stuck on the top. What does seem to be the case with his first guitars, is that the bridge did not have any saddles and the strings started from the holes.

Torres constructed guitars in two different periods: 1852–1869 (1st period) and 1875–1892 (2nd period). In describing guitars by Juan Moreno, scholar Aguado speaks of two instruments: the first with the fingerboard system that was flat on the top; the other (constructed in 1835) with the fingerboard superimposed on the top, bracing inside, and a saddle on the bridge.

Ten pegholes for five pairs of strings. Upper frets set into the soundboard, which is flush with the fingerboard. Coat of arms at base of fingerboard indicated instrument belonged to a noble family. Rosette carved in continuous intertwining scrollwork. Soundboard of pine and body of golden flamed maple. Back of peghead inscribed: ANT^S STRADIVARIUS CREMONON^S F 1680. At the time Hipkins' book was published (1888) this guitar was in the collection of W.E. Hill and Sons, London.

What I wonder is whether Antonio Torres laid hands on some of the last guitars constructed by Juan Moreno and if so, whether this helped him to establish his construction and create a school to establish the prototype for the modern guitar. If that was the case, which seems very likely to me, then it can be affirmed that Antonio Torres either earned his guitar construction know-how from his knowledge of the Madrid guitar-makers school, or it was sheer coincidence. What I can never doubt, or help admitting, is that the guitars constructed by Antonio Torres are the achievement, of the highest degree of guitar lutherie. His template designs, constant variations of the soundholes and rosettes, his permanent concern for the woods used, the perfection in his fingerboards, his ornamentation, and the beauty of his sound are just a few examples of his professionalism. Undoubtedly, he was a man of great personality who was able to earn the admiration and respect of the guitar music world of his time, and who left for us, the future generations, a splendid example to follow.

Hundreds of thousands of guitars were created in the world based on the construction system established by and attributed to Antonio Torres, and hundreds of thousands more will be manufactured in the future using his system. His achievements paved the way for the existence of a guitar with which the concert guitarist, from that time onwards, was able to raise the interest in this instrument, and thereby establish a pre-eminent place in the musical world of today and of the future. Once again, intuition, perception, and common sense at work.

Scientists the world over have put more interest in converting our guitar into an instrument of far-reaching sound. Most of them—the most qualified ones—acknowledge its complexity and admire and enjoy its beauty just as it is. Others call into question, a bit harshly, the skills of the guitar luthier with regards to the instrument's design and interior construction.

I have witnessed many such assessments and none of them are anything to write home about. At the end of the '60s, my distinguished friend, the eminent teacher Frederick Noad, was directing a program for teaching classical guitar on the Education and Culture channel in Hollywood. One fine day, as I was making my guitars in my own workshop at home, at 8410 West Third Street, I received a call from him asking if I would be interested in appearing on his program. Of course I was interested, and thanked him very much for his proposal. He told me I would be sharing the program with a certain scientist who had constructed a mathematically "perfect" guitar. For several days my workshop was invaded by cameras and flashes as I was filmed making my guitars. Then came the great day. The fact that I was appearing with my friend Fred Noad and this young scientist was a cherished experience. We chatted before the cameras, and the young scientist showed his guitar and mathematical graphs.

Guitar Pagés Cadiz 1790.

I do not want to judge this young scientist. The fact is, I am still constructing my guitars, and only God knows where this young scientist is today (this was about 30 years ago). Never again did I hear of him or of his guitars. Shortly before then, a Greek and a Latin-American had also designed a scientific guitar template of which I've heard nothing since.

In these last 40 years—even in my youthful years at the workshop where I worked with José Ramírez III (Pepe Jr. III, son of José Ramírez II) who, apart from being very skilful and artistic at the very few guitars he personally constructed, was one of the most curious and inquiring luthiers I have ever seen—the biggest ambition that united J.R. II and me (in addition to his bad temper) was to design the "perfect" guitar.

Various trials were made: different string scales, various star bracing crossed from the length and breadth of the soundboard, other modules and materials were introduced. The famous plastic ellipse, as in the ideal, cheerful, great hall of the El Escorial Monastery, was tried out. (There, if you whisper in one corner you are heard loud in the opposite corner. The idea was that if the bridge produced sound vibrations, the ellipse would reproduce it through the soundhole, boosting it. Another utopian dream.)

What was obvious was that nobody at the workshop had any true knowledge—not even pre-university knowledge, much less doctorates in physics and mathematics—just intuition, the inquisitiveness of a beginner, imagination, and a huge enthusiasm. Then several templates were constructed; one with a central point.

Of all these experiences and experiments, none of them was so bad as to be destroyed, or good enough to stand out and be pursued further.

Coming back to the many scientists who tried to improve on the luthier's craft, I recall one example in which such erudite gentlemen used a 650mm string scale, taking measurements, and making comparative physical, acoustic, and geometric trials with two famous A. Torres guitars crafted in 1864 and 1888. The results were quite insignificant. To me, the comparison was a banality. Science, with its curiosity to find out all about created objects, has for decades been questioning and assessing the concept of the stringed instruments designed in the 16th, 17th, and 18th centuries, as well as Torres's bracing, which runs semi-parallel to the grains of the wood and reinforces the parts of the soundboard where the string scale exerts the highest tension. This design is just the archetype of the profession.

But the luthier with certain professional standing, interest, and concern, designs his models to reflect the sound personality of the instrument with which he identifies himself. The professional, the inquisitive type, experiments with different designs of the interior structure of the soundboard, always depending on the quality of the wood he has in hand. His touch—absolutely essential—determines everything.

Logically, the soundboard, as in the case of other stringed instruments, was made from pinewood. Nowadays, good optimum-quality pinewood is becoming more and more scarce, which is why cedar wood and American pináceos have been used. (More about these in chapter 2).

In each quality wood, the professional luthier selects and designs the thickness and bracing, relying on his knowledge and experience. A greater number of the trials are carried out inside the soundboard. The strange thing is that, in general, the variations in these scientific experiments and designs are based on the changes in the design of the bracing.

With regard to guitar construction, scientists—every one of them, without exception—described the luthier's methods with a certain degree of scorn. In fact, given the enormous progress made within the guitar-making industry over the last 50 years, it must be remembered that all those who, from various viewpoints, have shown concern for the guitar, are all obsessed with enhancing its sound. On the one hand, there are the scientists with their calculations and theories; and on the other, the guitarists who, instead of striving to be better musicians, urge the luthiers to makes changes that deform the physiognomy of the guitar, whereupon the guitar ceases to be a guitar. And there are also the new luthiers who make holes on the soundboard as if it were Gruyère cheese, and then pose for a photograph with their novelty.

An infinity of new bracing designs comes out every day, and every luthier claims his is the best. If a novice guitarist finds it appealing, it is immediately recommended to him as if it were an absolute truth, whereas, in fact, we all imitate each other. As the saying goes: "If you merely imitate, you merely limit yourself." The compulsion to imitate is innate in all of us. "However, it is not easy to recognize what we must imitate," said Goethe. Well, the point is that, despite the fact that in our days we are attempting to create the finest instrument, the individual and unique experience of the luthier are huge factors that ensure that the guitar is born with beauty in sound and appearance.

Nowadays, everyone knows about the degradation that Mother Earth is suffering at the hands of humans. Our woods are burning, trees are being felled, and wood is being consumed at a higher rate than trees can be grown to replace it.

But what is certain is that guitars constructed today are far more resistant than those made 20 years ago. Today we have a greater number of varnishes and glues to protect the wood, the drying time is longer, and we use more time-tested methods in the construction of our guitars. The luthier's care can be seen in every section of the piece. With such materials, it comes as no surprise that the instrument has become a highly prized jewel, since it would serve as a source of knowledge for future generations, thanks to the precious woods and the painstaking care with which it has been created.

In this respect, scientists have an open field before them. I hope that they will demonstrate their talent by creating synthetic woods that look natural, and yet keep all the magical qualities that create unequalled sounds. This way we would, to some extent, both alleviate the shortage of wood and solve all acoustic and resonance problems, converting this instrument into a remarkable soloist in our orchestras, thanks to the volume of its sound. As Pertain, the illustrious Roman, would say: "Not everyone likes the same thing: some choose thorns while others, roses." Therein lies the scientific challenge to create incomparable roses.

After a lifetime of craftsmanship in my guitar-making career, I have discovered that what I wish above all else is, precisely, to establish various models of quality production, with different systems of construction and interior design that produce different quality sounds. This would be the way to provide the guitarist with the variety of sounds that we may have achieved. We would therefore be in a position to distinguish between the guitars that we like most, and so choose our own option of sound.

The true luthier artist is the one who has an intuition for shape and design, the one who respects the color of the wood and matches its natural aesthetics, the one who is concerned that the shape of the guitar form a beautiful whole with the design of the headstock finishings—finishings that identify and distinguish his instrument in the eyes of the public—and the one who is also concerned that his mosaic, purfling, and other incrustations have an aesthetic sense and clear-cut personality.

The genuine luthier is the one whose instrument does not look like anything that can be copied.

1.2. Madrid: The Capital of the Guitar. Guitar Makers' School from 1600 until Today.

When we take a look at the whole of the 15th century, we must point out the boost that the guitar and its composers enjoyed during the reign of Juan II in Spain. Juan de Palencia, Alfonso de Peñafiel (1414, "Master of Santiago's guitar player"), or Alfonso de Toledo and Martín de Toledo, the accomplished guitar minstrels who received the Navarra king's favour were just a few of the guitar's exponents.

In 1417, we had the remarkable figure of Rodrigo de la Guitarra, who served as a minister in the court of King Alfonso V of Aragón. Later he would go into the service of Juan II of Castilla (1405–1454). During this time, a festive ambience dominated the Madrid royal court; even King Juan II himself played the guitar, both for the solace of his court and for his own spiritual tranquillity.

Likewise, according to other information sources, in the Madrid jurisdiction in 1212, all the gentlemen who came into the city to strum charged a fee of three maravedíes. When the royal court was moved to Madrid, the guitar became popular among the nobility, and soon an ordinance was issued to regulate it. One of the first guilds in the capital was that of the Viola and Guitar Makers in 1578. In 1607, Juan de Carrión, viola maker, luthier, and harpist of the royal household, was a member of this guild. Prat shows details of bills paid to Juan de Carrión for constructing, repairing, and stringing guitars, harps, lyres, lutes, and violins. We do not have any more data on this character who must have lived between the last two decades of the 16th century and the first four of the 17th century. Today, however, as far as we know, there is no extant instrument by this master of lutherie.

In 1600, Spain was the European country where the vihuela and the guitar were mainly played. At that time, the plucking and strumming style was already in vogue, thus the reason why in Europe it was called the "hand vihuela," a name that distinguished our Spanish guitar.

In Madrid in 1695, gut strings were made for guitars. The strings had to be made from ram guts and not from any other animal.

According to the ordinances of viola makers in the 16th century, sixteen names were known in Madrid. Their number rose to forty in the 17th century. Such data is indicative of the intensity of the viola (guitar) making activities in the 16th and 17th centuries in the capital and the rest of Spain.

In Madrid, guitar makers were concentrated in areas around Angosta de Majaderitos, del Carmen Street and Carretas Street—all in the vicinity of La Puerta del Sol, the city center. The art and good workmanship of these guitar makers remain with us today, thanks to some well-preserved pieces. We know of other eminent contributors to the guitar of this period through references by teachers and concert guitarists who, in their methods and books, extolled the virtues of these guitars.

Actually, the age of the trade and the time at which these instruments were created are known, thanks to the labels on the guitars and the allusions made by guitarists of the period, who praised their works.

Juan de Carrión

Juan de Carrión was born in Madrid, possibly in 1587. In his dictionary, Prat gives an exhaustive account of his works as luthier, viola and guitar maker, harpist, repairer, and maker of period instruments, in the service of both Felipe III in the Royal Palace (1578–1621) and of Felipe IV (1606–1665).

Thanks to extensive documentation, bills, and budgets of the Royal Palace and National Wealth records, we have evidence of his great skills and know-how in working wood and other materials used in the construction of musical instruments. As already mentioned, it is unfortunate that, here in Spain, we do not know of any instrument made by him.

Marcos Antonio González

Judging by the typology of his guitar, we know that González settled in Madrid in 1766, on Majaderitos Street. He was the master of the Muñoa brothers, Manuel and Juan. Manuel married González's daughter and took over the workshop.

Lorenzo Alonso

A resident of Madrid, circa 1786 (data known thanks to his guitar), it is believed that between 1758 and 1788 Alonso had his workshop at 5 Carmen Street, where he died in 1796. In 1761 he was "overseer" (a name given in the guilds to the inspector who oversees the qualities and professionalism of guild members) of the Viola Makers of Madrid guild. It is also known that he awarded a professional examination certificate to his son, Pedro Alonso, when Pedro was only three years old, which discredited Alonso's system.

Lorenzo Alonso, who also constructed bowed stringed instruments, was mentioned by Fernando Sor in his *Méthode pour la guitarre*.

Benito Sánchez de Aguilera

A resident of Madrid, circa 1797 (date from his guitar), Sánchez de Aguilera was the guitar builder of Majaderitos Street. According to news of the period, in 1794 he had a guitar on sale that had "six strings."

The Muñoa Brothers: Juan and Manuel Muñoa

Manuel (1779–1815) and Juan (1783–1834) Muñoa were natives of a town in Burgos, Prado Luengo, with no background in or relationship with music. They must have belonged to Marcos Antonio González's workshop— Manuel as his apprentice first and later Juan as well. (Aguado speaks of the Muñoas in his book, *Escuela de la Guitarra*, 1820).

Other Muñoas: Gregorio Muñoa (1846), Juan Muñoa's son, and Antonio Muñoa (1820), Manuel Muñoa's son, (according to his guitar dated 1820). Manuel Muñoa married his master Marcos Antonio González's daughter. When Manuel died in 1825, his brother Juan married his widow (1827). Juan died in 1834.

Manuel Narciso González

A resident of Madrid, González must have lived between 1781 and 1847. He was the son of Marcos Antonio González and brother-in-law of the Muñoas. Upon Juan Muñoa's death in 1834, he took charge of the workshop on Majaderitos Street. The label on his guitar, dated 1833, reads "From the Royal Chamber to His Majesty."

Agustín o Benito Campo

A resident of Madrid, circa 1840, he was a great collaborator of the old master Dionisio Aguado. Following Manuel Narciso González's death, Agustín took over the Muñoas' workshop on Majaderitos Street.

Diego Sánchez

The label on Sánchez's guitar states: "Composed by Diego Sánchez, Madrid 1837."

Juan Moreno

Moreno settled in Madrid on Majaderitos Street. He was born in 1792 and died in 1836, at the age of 44. According to Dionisio Aguado's testimony, the Madrid guitar makers of the first 26 years of the 19th century broke away from the construction standard of that time, taking as their benchmark the guitars constructed in 1829 by Juan Moreno. The oldest known guitar thought to be Moreno's was made in line with the traditional standards used until then. The reinforcements of the inside of his soundboard comprised three transverse struts, one on each side of the soundhole and the third beneath the bridge. The joint was reinforced with a strip of wood, the fingerboard on the same level as the soundboard. The frets up to the 12th were on the rosewood fingerboard, and from the 12th to the 18th were incrusted on the soundboard. The bridge was a 1.5 centimeter stick, in which there were holes that held the strings towards the fingerboard. This guitar had six double strings.

This change in Juan Moreno's guitar, dated 1830, already gave it the appearance and construction of subsequent guitars. The fingerboard was a single piece on the neck, and the soundboard, slightly curved, had six strings. On the bridge, the strings already rested on a saddle, and two transverse struts, fixed at both sides of the soundhole, formed the inside of the soundboard. The most curious thing was that on the broader part of the soundboard and the bridge area, this guitar already had five bracings, with the broadest one in the center. This detail makes us assume that this guitar maker was innovative as far as the fan system in the soundboard is concerned, prefiguring even Torres, whose fan bracing in his guitar "La Leona" (1856) was similar. His predecessors in Madrid also used these new methods: the Muñoas, M. N. González, F. González, and J. Ramírez, who constructed a guitar entirely from maple, including the top.

Francisco González

Born in Corgomo (Orense) in 1820 (d. 1879), F. González died in Madrid. He arrived in Madrid in 1836, at the age of sixteen. Among the famous and prestigious guitar makers in Madrid at that time were Manuel Narciso González (it is not known if they were related), Juan Muñoa, Gregorio Muñoa, and Antonio Muñoa. F. González could well have entered into the workshops of any of these masters as an apprentice, which all goes to show that the Madrid school was already consolidated.

Other guitar makers established in Madrid who could also have initiated F. González into the trade were Agustín (according to a guitar of Madrid 1840) and Diego Sánchez (Madrid, 1860).

In 1860, F. González ran his own workshop at 40 Toledo Street, which makes us think that in those 24 years in Madrid he must have been working at other guitar-making workshops. In 1861, he moved a bit closer to the center, to Carrera de San Jerónimo Street (possibly to start his apprenticeship here in 1870, where the other master of masters, José Ramírez, started at twelve). In 1890, he moved yet again, to 33 Carretas Street, the final move made by the firm. He must have died very old, at the beginning of the 20th century.

I met his son-in-law, Enrique Romano—a real trader of his time, very arrogant with his finances, and more interested in guitars from the factory in Valencia than in the handcrafted ones from Madrid.

F. González's two daughters followed him into his trade. He had a likeable manager, Santiago Collado, who was a fine banduria player and a good friend of my father's and Marcelo Barbero's. In those years he was moonlighting after his day's work at Ramírez's, doing repair work at González's workshop. I gave him a helping hand; my father did the varnishing. That was the tough decade of the '40s.

Vicente Arias

Born in Ciudad Real in 1840, he died in Madrid in 1912, at 72. Arias's first guitars were dated in Ciudad Real around 1874; his last ones were constructed in Madrid at 20 Santa Isabel Street.

In my modest collection, I am really proud to possess a guitar by Vicente Arias, dated Madrid 1904, at 4 Álamo Street.

Antonio Carracedo

A resident of Madrid, circa 1860, Carracedo crafted guitars that are commended in Toma's Damas's method.

José Ramírez-Galarreta Planell: J. R. the First

Born in Madrid in 1858, J.R. I died in 1923 at the age of 65. When he was twelve years old (1820) he joined Francisco González's workshop on San Jerónimo Street as an apprentice. He set up his own workshop at the early age of 24, on what is today Rivera de Curtidores Street, then moved in 1890 to 2 Concepcion Jerónimo Street in Madrid. His brother, Manuel Ramírez—who subsequently became a great master—worked in both of these workshops, as did Enrique García, Rafael Casana, Julián Gómez Ramírez, and Antonio Viudes. The Ramírezes were and still are a living example of the enterprising spirit. Upon attaining maturity in the trade, they set up workshops, took on workers, and trained them. This was the real vocation of Ramírez and his brother Manuel and, up to now, that of the Ramírezes' generation.

Only God knows if the Madrid guitar makers' school would have survived

José Ramirez I (1858–1923)   José Ramírez II (1885–1957)   José Ramirez III

without the Ramirezes; although I myself was aware of José Ramírez II's intention, in the 1940s, of closing down his workshop so as to capitalize on the
nascent guitar industry in Valencia.

Working in J. Ramírez's workshop during his last years were handymen
Alfonso Benito, Antonio Gómez, my father Manuel Rodríguez, who also varnished the guitars, and Marcelo Barbero, who worked as an apprentice.

With the death of José Ramírez in 1923, and until the return of his son, José
Ramírez II, from Argentina in 1925, the workshop was managed by his handymen. The shop was run by his daughters and a dynamic technician-cum-musician
shop assistant called Jesús Martínez (father of the current manager of the firm)
until his death in the '60s. Martinez was a wonderful person and a fine mandolin
player; in short, a great musician. He met my father during his youthful years in
Paris before World War I, a time when Spanish musicians enjoyed prestige with
their stringed orchestras. He was a good companion and loyal to the firm.

On his return, José Ramírez II bought his siblings' share of the business
and took full control of it. The times that José Ramírez lived in Spain were
turbulent ones. The monarchy was in a precarious situation, the economy
shaky and unstable. In those years, guitars, bandurias, and lutes only sold at
the end of the harvest seasons and at Christmas, given that these instruments
were favoured by the groups of serenaders that formed in little towns and
in provinces. The summer was the time for constructing these instruments
for subsequent sales. Maestro Ramírez found it rather hard to maintain the
workshop, store the guitars, and pay workers during the lean seasons.

I have the fondest memory of and also respect for Maestro José Ramírez
I, thanks to all that I was told by my father, who held him in high esteem and
consideration. He was always referring to the master as a good professional
and a great person.

Manuel Ramírez (1864–1916)

The Ramírez's successors:

Amalia Ramírez

José Enrique Ramírez IV
(1953–2000)

Manuel Ramírez-Galarreta Planell

Born in Alhama in Aragón in 1864, Manuel learned the trade from his brother José, six years older than he, in the Cava Baja workshop around 1882. The story goes that Manuel, a good guitar handyman and a good disciple of his brother, but concerned about his future, sought advice and help from his brother in order to set up his own business. José complied, for in his original plans, Manuel was to set up a guitar-making workshop in the city of "light and illusion of Europe," Paris. Only God knows why Manuel changed his mind and stayed in Madrid. When his brother José learned of this, he must have been truly offended, as they did not exchange words ever again in their lifetimes.

So, Manuel Ramírez opened his workshop at 5 Santa Ana Square, only a dozen blocks away from José's. Manuel differentiated his guitar construction from his brother's with distinctive features that characterized him as a fervent follower of the school of Torres.

Over time, a marked difference was established between the guitars built at the workshops of each of these brothers. José continued with his experience and traditions, whilst Manuel, by contrast, was more committed to the guitar and to the most contemporary school of Antonio Torres, in which he must have found a much broader horizon. Consequently, his workshop in those days was considered to be the natural successor of the school of Torres.

Manuel Ramírez was an inquisitive researcher and a skilful craftsman. Torres's idea was copied and further developed at his workshop. Ramírez was a remarkable violin luthier and enjoyed prestige during his epoch.

Graduating from his workshop and under his tutorship were several accomplished guitar makers who honored Ramírez with their professionalism: Enrique García, who set up shop in Barcelona; Domingo Esteso, a painstaking craftsman who perfectly mastered woodwork and demonstrated throughout his prolific production the high quality of his guitars, earning the admiration of the professional guitarist (it was not for nothing that the quality of his instruments, guitars, lutes, and bandurias served as an example for professional serenader troupes in the '20s and the '30s); and Modesto Borreguero, the youngest, who was also an expert guitar craftsman.

Perhaps his most outstanding follower, both on account of the prestige attained as well as of his own skills, was Santos Hernández. Like his master before him, Hernández was a faithful follower of Torres, as well as a great violin luthier.

Manuel Ramírez left no descendants, as he had no children. He died in Madrid on 25 February 1916.

Jose Ramirez II and III in the 1950s

José Ramirez III

José Ramirez III

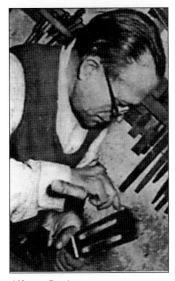

Alfonso Benito

Manuel Rodriguez, in his 20s

Manuel Rodriguez, in his 20s

Agustín Andrés

A guitar-making guitarist, A. Andrés had his workshop in Madrid, on Manuel Fernández y González Street, next to Santa Ana Square. In this neighborhood—right in the center of Madrid, a guitar area with a flamenco ambience—is the spot where guitar makers in the closing years of the 19th century and the beginning of the 20th century were based.

I should know more about A. Andrés, since my father told me that Andrés was his first workshop. My grandfather, on a visit to this craftsman's workshop, and aware that my father was in need of a profession, asked Maestro Andrés if he, by any chance, needed a helper. As you can imagine, the answer was affirmative. So my father entered the workshop as an apprentice at 18, when J. Gómez Ramírez was the first handyman. This must have been in the spring of 1905. In 1907 Andrés moved to Paris and set up his workshop at 7 Puteaux Street. (Prat met him in Paris in 1910). A. Andrés died in 1913.

Antonio Viudes

Born in Crevillente (Alicante) on 10 November 1883, he arrived in Madrid at the age of 14, in 1897. He worked as an apprentice at Manuel Ramírez's workshop from 1897 to 1902. Later on, he moved to work at the shop of José Ramírez I. He left for Buenos Aires in 1909, and died in 1930.

I had a beautiful banduria with buttons made by this guitar maker.

Saturnino Rojas

S. Rojas (1859–1937) was a guitar builder established in Madrid at 115 Atocha Street. He was a contemporary in his early years of Ramírez, and in his latter years of F. González, Santo Hernández, and Esteso.

I got to know Saturnino Rojas when he was very old, in the years just before the Civil War. The most characteristic thing about him was that the labels on his guitars had his portrait, in which he sported a beautiful moustache.

He was a very good friend of my father's, who did his varnishing and helped him in his work and business. He never married, but instead lived with a sister in a flat in the same building as the workshop. At the beginning of 1936, my father and Marcelo Barbero were negotiating to take possession of the workshop. I can even remember, if my memory serves me right, that he was asking for about 7,000 pesetas. But then the war entered our lives and that put an end to everything. A living case of "man proposes and God disposes."

When we returned in 1939, Saturnino, who died in 1937, and his guitar-making workshop had disappeared. His school could well have been that of González, Torres, or Ramírez.

Valentín Viudes, Father and Son

The Viudes settled in Madrid in the Ribera de Curtidores in the middle of the 1800s. Santos Hernández is said to have entered as an apprentice with Valentín Viudes Jr.

Julián Gómez Ramírez

J. G. Ramírez was born in Madrid on 22 May 1879, and died in Paris in 1948. He must have started off in the trade as an apprentice with José Ramírez in the last years of the century. He was, as was customary, very young. J. Gómez, M. Ramírez and E. García worked alongside him as co-disciples at José Ramírez's workshop on Ribera de Curtidores Street.

Years later he passed through Antonio Viudes's workshop as a handyman, and also worked at Agustín Andrés's workshop in Fernán y González Street, close to Santa Ana Square, where my father started as apprentice in 1905. He could be said to have been my father's first master.

At the time of the Universal Exhibition of 1899, Paris was the focal point of Europe and the world. Its appeal was enlightening and it charmed those near and far alike. M. Ramírez dreamt of moving to Paris but could not make up his mind, whereas Agustín Andrés and Julián Gómez did make the move. Once in Paris, they could not have been together for long, seeing that Andrés settled at 7 Puteaux Street, whereas Julián went to 38 Rodier Street, where he worked until his death. In 1958, I had confirmation of this from a customer of mine and a friend of Julián's, Jesús Ruiz, a Spanish guitar teacher, in a letter I still have in which he mentioned that Julián's widow, Anjel, was still alive in those days.

My father went to work with him again at the workshop on Rodier Street. They constructed guitars, as well as lutes, bandurias, and mandolins. Naturally, the guitars constructed by my father at this workshop all bore the name of the master. My father returned to Spain with his family in 1914, at the advent of World War I. Julián continued his business in Paris, consolidating the crafts-manship he had acquired at the Madrid guitar-makers' school.

Julián was a fondly loved colleague and master, judging from the fondest memories my father had of him and their friendship, of which I am familiar from the countless anecdotes that he told me about their life together in that city, where Julián and his wife lived together with his brothers. My father thought highly of them until his death; hence my most devoted respect for such an illustrious colleague.

Julián Ramírez must have died in the year 1948.

Enrique García Castillo

Born in Madrid in 1868, Castillo died in Barcelona on 31 October 1922. He started off at Manuel Ramírez's workshop, in Santa Ana Square. From this workshop experience, and thanks to his great craftsmanship, he won the first prize at the Chicago Exposition in 1893. García continued another two years with M. Ramírez, and then moved in 1895 to Barcelona. His first years in this city, where he set up shop on Aragón Street, were not easy at all. Nevertheless, given his professionalism and the recognition received from experts in Catalonia, his guitars were highly valued.

García was a good friend and protégé of Domingo Prat, who for many years had promoted his guitars in Argentina. Today, these instruments, like those of the great masters before him, are truly appreciated and have become highly prized collectors' pieces.

He left behind a disciple, Francisco Simplicio, whose guitars are another great example of our lutherie art, which he consolidated in Barcelona, setting examples for other to follow.

Francisco Simplicio was born in Barcelona on 18 October 1874 and died in the same city on 14 January 1933.

Rafael Casana

We do not have much information about this craftsman. It is known that he learned the trade from José Ramírez and Antonio Viudes when they were working together with M. Ramírez and Julián Gómez. When Antonio Viudes left for Argentina, Rafael Casana, a handyman by then, set up shop in the Andalusian city of Córdoba.

It is assumed—and I can neither confirm nor refute this—that he was the master of Miguel Rodríguez, who hailed from Córdoba.

I met Miguel Rodríguez at the end of the 1940s, when he was already old. He is today succeeded by his children and grandchildren in Córdoba.

By sheer chance, we share the same surname Rodríguez, but we are in no way related. There are millions of Rodríguezes in this country. What is true, however, is that my parents are natives of Cádiz, whereas Miguel Rodríguez was from Córdoba; both are in Andalusia.

I do not know any guitar by Casana, but I do as far as his disciple Miguel Rodríguez is concerned. And I must say that all my due respect goes to this great master.

Santos Hernández Rodríguez

S.H. Rodríguez was born in Madrid in 1873 and died there in 1942 (reference: Prat). At the age of ten (1883) he started working at Valentín Viudes Jr.'s workshop on Ribera de Curtidores Street (the flea market area). He worked for some time in the workshops of Ortega and Saturnino Rojas. According to my father, he did his military service in 1893, when he was 20, and stayed there for five years, until 1898. Upon graduation, he was already an adult and a full-fledged professional. He must have been self-employed at a workshop that he set up on Nicolas Salmerón Street, Madrid. This is what is recorded in any case, on a guitar of his successors of the workshop and another owned by Maestro Áureo Herrero of Madrid.

Thus, in 1905, Santos Hernández started at Manuel Ramírez's workshop as first handyman, in replacement of Enrique García, who had then moved to Barcelona. An artist craftsman noted for his dignity and perfectionism, he gave Manuel Ramírez's workshop such a boost that it became the most prestigious of his time.

Santos was the one who built the guitar used by the grand master Segovia in his concerts for over 25 years, which gave Segovia access to the most prestigious auditoriums around the world and earned him the applause of all audiences. This guitar must have been created, under professional inspiration, with a good choice of wood, with the highest sensitivity of touch, hearing, and sight that every now and then opens up a shutter in the intelligence and spirit. This guitar has been the masterpiece of our trade, and the fact that with it Segovia delighted his audiences has served to make it the paradigm for makers from other countries who, thanks to it, have years later developed their own models.

Santos Hernández must have been the Ramírez's first handyman and right-hand man, for when he started working at this workshop in 1905, he was already 32, and had passed through several workshops. He worked for himself and took over the post of manager and first handyman vacated by Enrique García. Domingo Esteso and Modesto Borreguero must have been working at this workshop already. The age difference (7 years older than Esteso and 19 years older than Borreguero), coupled with his experience, made him the master of the workshop. For sure, he must have helped Ramírez a lot in his violin lutherie, given that years later he became an expert repairman of this instrument. He really must have had a lot of prestige because, when he died, his widow had to hire a luthier to repair the violins that were sent to his workshop.

Manuel Ramírez died at an early age of 52, in 1920. Back then his workshop was at 8 Arlabán Street. Santos, Esteso, and Borreguero stayed on at the workshop, using the name of Manuel Ramírez's widow. Each of these guitar makers appended their initials on the corner of the label inside the guitar.

Flamenco guitar by
Santos Hernandez,
Madrid 1924.

In 1921, Santos Hernández set his up own workshop again (which is run today by his present successors at 24 Aduana Street). I do not know when he married. He did not have any children and therefore no direct descendants. Those running the workshop today are nephews of his wife, Matilde.

I got to know Maestro Santos Hernández in my childhood, before our damn Civil War. My father was working with him from the time he set up shop in Aduana Street, where more often than not my father did the varnishing on the Maestro's guitars. Both of them were kind-hearted and good-natured, and my father openly professed a genuine admiration for Maestro Santos Hernández's person and works. I firmly believe that all his life my father felt a sincere affection towards Santos; I am also aware that Santos felt likewise towards him.

In the years until his death, Santos's guitar was the indisputable instrument among professionals in the world. In flamenco circles, the Santos guitar was the ultimate guitar. Masters of that art played his guitar—which provided part of Santos's income in his old age, thanks to the exorbitant price paid for this instrument. Santos, like almost every luthier of our time until the '60s, constructed more flamenco guitars than concert guitars; for in Spain flamenco was where guitar professionalism was.

The master luthier and guitar maker died in Madrid in 1942.

Santos was, in the words of Regino Sainz de Maza, "the Priest of the Craft." He would closely inspect the grains of the wood as he observed how they dried and became finer, hoping that a lyric wind would make them sing.

Personally, I consider Maestro Santos Hernández to be the master of modern guitar, after Antonio Torres. Like Torres, he felt concern for improving the instrument and never settled for anything less. He never repeated the same mosaic and veneer on his soundholes (all his soundholes were different). Like Torres, he created and experimented with different string scales, bracings, and varnishes. Like Torres, and more than any other luthier of his time, he sought the perfection of our flamenco and concert guitar. At the Alfil Bookshop (no longer in existence) on Arenal Street, years after his death, Santos's widow and friends organized, in tandem with the nascent Madrid Guitar Society, an exhibition of his guitars in 1945. On display were all the Santos guitars. His friends gave concerts and lectures. As far as I remember, Regino Sainz de la Maza, Pedro Moreno, the Martínez sisters América and España, and the Exquembre Trio played, as did a flamenco guitarist. It was memorable and delightful to dedicate such a well-deserved homage to the indisputable master. To me, it was a beautiful memorial. It was also a pity that there was no chance to say a few words in honor of a luthier who left, as a souvenir and to the delight of his fellow men, no less than a musical instrument. Let there be another commemoration! This happened at a given time and in a given moment, and it was organized by endearing people.

But... Thank you, Santos, for living and making guitars.

Myself.

Santos Hernandez

Santos Hernandez descendants: Messr. Santos Bayon and son during a visit. I paid them for an article that appeared in the *Classical Guitar* magazine.

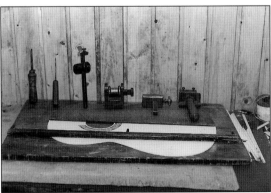

Maestro Santos Hernandez's working bench and tools.

Domingo Esteso López

Born in San Clemente (Cuenca) on 12 May 1882, López died in Madrid in the year 1937, in the midst of the Civil War. Domingo Esteso is not known to have worked in any other workshop where he could have learned as an apprentice. He must have started off in the trade as an apprentice at Manuel Ramírez's shop at a very early age. Could it have been in the closing years of the century? Manuel Ramírez had just set up his own shop a few years back, so López must have been one of his very first disciples. He stayed at the workshop until the death of the master, and continued working with his widow until the workshop closed down in 1917.

That same year, Domingo Esteso set up a workshop at the present address (7 Gravina Street), the parent workshop, where the master died. For 20 years he lived there and taught the trade to his three nephews: Faustino, Mariano, and Julio Conde.

Domingo was a great master guitar craftsman. He constructed fantastic concert and flamenco guitars, as well as lutes and bandurias. He produced a great number of instruments, for he was hard-working and highly productive. Today his guitars are greatly valued by professionals and are the envy of numerous collectors.

After his death, Domingo's widow carried on the business with his nephews, changing the name from Domingo Esteso to Hermanos Conde, after Domingo Esteso's nephews. Three professionals dedicated to guitar construction, the Conde brothers were more productive than their uncle was. They even set up a workshop of a considerable size, where, with the help of some assistants, they produced medium-quality guitars.

The three brothers, Faustino, Mariano, and Julio, personally constructed their guitars, which were aimed at flamenco professionals—a sector where they enjoyed, and still do, a good deal of admiration.

Today, the workshop is run by Julio Conde, Faustino Conde's widow, Julio Conde and Mariano's children, Felipe and Mariano Conde.

Modesto Borreguero

Born in Madrid in 1894, Borreguero died on 23 June 1969. He was the least famous handyman in Maestro Manuel Ramírez's workshop when the latter's widow closed it down in 1920. He was also the youngest in that small-sized company.

I met Maestro Borreguero in the years just before our wretched Civil War, when he had the workshop at 5 Nuñez de Arce Street. In those years, my father also varnished the Maestro's instruments. According to his disciple and friend, Vicente Camacho, "He was the typical chatty Madrid native, good-humoured and fond of our wines." He was painstaking in his creation of instruments for serenader groups. Given his bohemian nature, he had many workshops. After a crisis, he was admitted, out of consideration, at the workshop of master cabinetmakers Aguado and Hernández, on Ribera de Curtidores Street. Upon seeing him make his guitars, they soon learned the mechanism of the trade, and thanks to their cabinetmaking professional know-how, they became high-standard guitar makers—not to mention the added help they received from the masters of the Madrid Conservatory.

It is difficult to find guitars by Maestro Borreguero today. He spent his last years making repairs and constructing one or two guitars at the workshop set up for him at the Garrido Recording House, next to his most loyal disciple, Vicente Camacho. He died in 1969, leaving behind a son, who would work with José Ramírez III.

Marcelo Barbero García

Marcelo García was born in 1904 and died in Madrid in 1959, at the age of 55. He joined Ramírez's workshop in April 1939, for the second time. At the death of José Ramírez I, and in 1923, Marcelo Barbero, who was then 19, was already working at this workshop. He stayed with José Ramírez III until 1930, when he started working on his own in his flat at 6 Ministriles Street, 1st floor left door. Years later, he moved to 1st floor, right door in the same building, where he lived until his death.

We lived in the same building, on the third floor, first door on the left. He lived with us, on a half-board arrangement, having lunch and supper with us until he got married in 1935. In 1936, the Civil War began and he was called up. We saw each other again after the war, in 1939. He worked freelance, and his guitars, bandurias, and lutes—popular instruments in Madrid and its provinces—earned him well-deserved fame among the many troupes of serenaders and orchestras who performed in the bars, taverns, and flamenco clubs that gave Madrid its unique character.

At the end of this stupid and bloody Civil War—stupid because of how wretched the motives were, and bloody on account of the carnage between people who shared the same language and historical identity—we all had to start over again with a shortage of absolutely everything. In the company where we worked, the first handyman took home 13 pesetas a day; Marcelo Barbero, 11 pesetas; my father, then a varnisher, 9; and I, 1.50 pesetas. A bar of bread (French stick) cost one peseta at that time on the black market.

Those years, as precarious as they were, already smacked of the future World War that would plunge Europe into total collapse. In our Spain, most

Marcelo Barbero; Madrid. 1954.
This photo was taken for
publicity and also upon the
request of certain friends.

of the basic goods were rationed. (Bread was rationed at 125g per day per head. If I am going on and on about details of these vicissitudes, it is only to underline our vocation; for during the time I am referring to, most people sought better opportunities, a change of trade, or jobs, in pursuit of something that was rewarding—materially, intellectually, and spiritually. The money we earned in this trade brought us nothing but precariousness. But therein lies the love for the work we did; the huge satisfaction of making a guitar, which was nothing less than an instrument that makes music. In the 1940s, when I started doing my daily tasks—12 guitars at a go—a guitar was selling for between 125 and 150 pesetas to the general public.

But getting back to Marcelo Barbero: while still working for Ramírez, he continued with his own workshop at Ministriles Street, where he did repair work and made one or two instruments, but not without a serious confrontation with his boss. As a result, he gradually started getting back his old customers and stepping up his work at his workshop. In 1941, he left Ramírez's and joined González's workshop on Carretas Street until 1944, when Santos Hernández's widow proposed that he work at that famous artist's workshop.

It was then that Barbero made contact with Santos Hernández's style of working, taking over the templates, tools, woods, and other working styles of the master. I know for sure that Marcelo never got to work with Santos; they had only met once at a guitar concert. However, this did not stop him, after Hernández's death, from becoming one of his disciples, inheriting the skills of the master whom he followed.

During the time we worked at Ramírez's, Benito was first handyman; my father, Manuel Rodríguez, the varnisher; Ramón Peñalver, apprentice; and myself the second handyman. As production was shrinking, my father worked with Marcelo at the Santos workshop on a temporary basis. Santos's widow completed her workforce with the addition of one self-taught beginner and a violin luthier—today a renowned master, Fernando Solar, native of Orense. (In the photograph on page 39, the three of us are standing at the door of the Santos Hernández Guitar Making Workshop.)

Marcelo worked with Santos's widow until the '50s, combining this work with the work he did at his workshop on Ministriles Street. By then he already had two children: Alicia, who was born in 1936 and who died in the 1980s; and Marcelo, who was born at the end of the 40s and is today an outstanding luthier.

Marcelo lived out his life's dream, fulfilling his vocation at the Santos Hernández workshop. From every sphere of the guitar-making industry he received recognition—from professional concert guitarists to amateurs who made up the influential Madrid Guitar Society.

It is strange that "minstrel," etymologically speaking, refers to a person who saw to the less-important affairs of Justice; the person who played a wind instrument during ecclesiastical moments.

In the last five years of his life, Marcelo began to have serious health problems. He never was a strong man. During and after the war, we went through a period of need—food and medicines were lacking, and many could not make it through. Marcelo was a vegetarian for most of his life and a man with a lot of responsibilities in his work. In the '50s he became very popular all over the world, and orders for his guitars shot up dramatically. He earned a lot of prestige especially in the flamenco field. This excess of work might have undermined his health. He was falling behind on his orders and it caused him a great deal of concern and desperation. His illness, which, ominously, stretched into weeks, brought him close to that fateful day of 6 March 1956. I wish these words to serve as homage to my colleague and bosom friend. We lived together as family in the same flat, and shared the same professional address. I only want to say that anyone who makes such beautiful, handcrafted guitars as Marcelo did has a great value in the professional world. He never had any machine whatsoever; not even a mechanical tool. His tools were the same as those used in biblical times. With his specially cared-for woods, and a lot of sacrifice, he constructed guitars in which he left part of his life.

Madrid 1944–45. Gate of the Santos Hernandez Workshop at 53 Aduana Street. From left to right: Marcelo Barbero, my father, and Fernando Solar, the violin luthier.

Manuel Díaz Hernández and Victoriano Aguado

The main occupation of Hernández (1895–1975) and Aguado (1897–1980) was that of working in a quality cabinetmaking shop, where they repaired furniture and pianos, and varnishing them as well.

Their workshop was at 7 Ribera de Curtidores, in the inner storehouse of an 18th-century tenement building. At the end of the 1940s, the bohemian Borreguero was left without a workshop or premises where his working bench and wood could be set up. As he had lived in neighborhoods around the center of Madrid (Lavapiés, El Rastro), Borreguero knew the cabinetmakers Aguado and Hernández. At that time, Madrid was just a little town—you could get to every place on foot, and everything was closer and more intimate. Therefore, faced with hardship and need, Maestro Borreguero must have asked these cabinetmakers to give him a room to work in. Aguado and Hernández, good wood professionals as they were, could have had a curiosity of guitar construction as well as a certain affinity, considering that they had done some work on pianos. Since they had extra space in the workshop, they welcomed Borreguero into their premises. Borreguero was thus able to continue making his instruments and be gainfully employed. All this must have happened at the end of the '40s, for the master was, at the beginning of the 1950s, working at the Garrido workshop, in Desengaño Street. From this tripartite relationship, both cabinetmakers developed expertise in guitar construction.

In those years, the world was already experiencing a rude awakening to the hell and wounds of the war; yet there was a certain yearning for knowing and developing new musical experiences. The demand for guitars was beginning to be noted. As a result, Aguado and Hernández, given their good name as cabinetmakers, were asked by the Madrid Conservatory to build several large luxury showcases made of top-quality wood and with considerable marquetry, which would exhibit a collection of guitars used by prestigious musicians. There on display were the guitars of the world-famous Mariano Cubas (a photograph of it can be seen on page 269 of Ivor Mairants's book, *My Fifty Fretting Years*), and another guitar belonging to Professor Regino Sainz Maza.

As a result of the success and recognition they earned from the creation of the two Madrid Conservatory guitar showcases, they were admitted into the Madrid Guitar Society.

De una materia triste,
sin carne seca,
dicen que amanecieron
sonidos, cuerda.
De una materia viva
—manos del hombre—
cítaras y vihuelas,
cadencias y sones,
y ¡la guitarra!
de las armas del cante
la más bizarra.
Prima y bordón:
alegría, tristeza,
ritmo y canción.
De una materia muerta,
¿será leyenda?
Nos llegaste, armonía,
con tus seis cuerdas.
Y el corazón
prestándote la angustia
de su dolor.
Transmutaciones…
de una materia muerta,
¡Todos los sones!

Eugenio D'Ors

1.3 My Family: Starting from My Flamenco Grandparents. My Father, Our Fairs, Our Workshops, and Our Professional Careers.

My Father: Manuel Rodríguez Pérez

My father was born on San Fernando Island (Cádiz) on 4 March 1887, the son of Manuel Rodríguez Marequi and Josefa Pérez Cano—both natives of the island. My father was the third of my grandparents' six children: Paco (1883), Manuela (1885), my father (1887), Joselito (1890), Antonia (1894), and Luisa (1990).

From the little I can recall of what my father told me, my grandfather came from a family whose fortunes had changed for the worse, and he must have learned to play the guitar as a hobby first. He would later become a real professional in the guitar trade. Before getting married to my grandmother, he must have lived the bohemian flamenco life of his day. My grandmother came from the middle-class Pérez trading family, wholesalers of some standing in San Fernando. One thing my father always boasted of was the love my grandparents had for each other.

Flamenco artists of their time and city, my grandparents also tried their hands at selling the typical fried fish; but fortune did not smile at them in this business.

At the dawn of the 19th century, a frigate—I believe a German one—arrived at the coast of Cádiz, and for some unknown reason sank some distance off the humble Cádiz port. There was a wild storm and the fury of the sea did not respect the solid frigate or the German sailors, who lost their lives on the Spanish coast. It was the biggest tragedy at the time. As a result of the consternation and horror caused by the drowning of so many human beings, the worthy inhabitants of the Bay of Cadiz and its surrounding area refrained from eating fish for months. The fried fish business sank, and its owners, my grandparents, were drowned economically. (This incident, recounted to me by my father, has been confirmed by the Naval Ministry through my friend Tovar in Germany, who checked on the veracity of the story). Given the circumstances, my grandfather returned to his guitar-making, and my grandmother to her dancing.

My grandfather must have been born around 1850. He must have been a good flamenco guitarist, seeing that he played at the most prestigious singing cafés in the whole of Andalusia. Ample technical knowledge was required of guitarists who played for and accompanied such artists while they sang and danced. He must have been a good musician too.

In the period when flamenco was booming, the flamenco clubhouses, known as los tablaos, in which my grandparents worked, had a totally differ-

The Manuel Rodriguez Marequi and Josefa Perez Family. Photo taken after the death of Josefa's mother.
L to R: Luisa, Paco, Joselito, my father Manolo, and Antoni. Seated is Manuel Rodriguez.
The eldest daughter, Manuela, does not appear in the photo.

ent scenography. In Granada there was a very important hall with capacity for 1,500 spectators—500 seated in the stalls and 1,000 in the stands, boxes, and stalls. That was in 1898.

In his trips around Europe—before World War I and during his stay in Paris—my grandfather had the opportunity to get to know other theatres. These had rows of seats with side tables attached to each, where spectators took their seats and helped themselves to some coffee or a glass of wine. In the boxes, one had to drink at least one bottle of wine, which meant that as new spectators arrived, the festive atmosphere would keep soaring from bottle to bottle. The flamenco mood and excitement obliged them to continue the celebration. They would choose a number of artists, singers, dancers, guitarists, and a joker or two, and would continue drinking and eating the snacks known as tapas.

My uncle, Joselito Rodriguez Marequi, my father's young brother. An outstanding flamenco guitarist and for many years the boyfriend and guitar accompanist of the famous, and now legendary, Dña Pastora Pavon.

In these singing cafés, the star was always the singer or the dancer. The guitarist was merely an accompanist. There were no rehearsals; the guitarist knew his job and would keep perfectly to the beat of the songs and the dances.

The stage consisted of a very wide platform decorated with mirrors and typical motifs (bullfighting posters and monuments such as The Giralda, The Golden Tower, etc.) and chairs on which the artists sat, toward the back, while the spectators moved their chairs forward towards the center of the tablao as they arrived.

Pepe, "the matron's son," comments on how exhausting the artist's job was. As he recalls his work in the Café del Gato in Madrid: "In this café, which was very small, we had to perform four times. First, you would sing with the women on stage. To learn the song, they would sing part of the song, then they would sing alone. Precisely when one sang alone, you would have one lady on each side and then the players. Later you would sing in the rooms. So there were days when one would leave at 12 noon. We were the last to leave. Alcohol would be flowing! And at 8 pm, we were back again. This was the case if you worked in the café, while others were more interested in having a good time. In such cases, the partying lasted for days." In the Madrid of my youth, there were both the tablaos and the colmaos, with a flamenco air, in which you could have drinks with tapas, and one easily got into a festive mood.

The Madrid colmaos became places of quality flamenco as well as tourist attractions, thanks to the presence of the best artists of the time. Nowadays, these singing cafés thrive more from tourism than from the rich aficionados who want to go partying.

It would be a fallacy, and a mistake as well, to classify all flamenco artists as rascals leading promiscuous lives. I knew of many who were respectably married and exemplary fathers who worked hard to provide for their children. My father's family was totally patriarchal. My grandfather, who was in love with his wife and was in turn loved by her, would, with a mere look, curb any unbecoming behavior by a son or daughter.

His youngest son, Joselito Rodríguez (Marequi) was a great professional. He was a guitarist and the boyfriend of the immortalized singing legend, La Niña de los Peines, whom he accompanied at a number of concerts in France. He died at an early age.

My father's sisters formed a successful dancing trio. They married early. His eldest brother, Paco, died while he was a civil servant with the Madrid City Council. He was neither a guitarist nor a singer.

My father's life as a professional guitar maker began in 1905 when he was 18, when he started working as an apprentice at Agustín Andrés's workshop, in Manuel Fernández and González alley in Madrid. At that time, Julián Gómez Ramírez, who became José Ramírez I's first handyman, worked in that guitar workshop.

The Marequi family moved to Paris around 1908. That was the time Agustín Andrés and Julián Gómez R. also arrived in the French city. My father started working at Julián Gómez R.'s workshop and remained there until 1914, when just as World War I broke out, he returned to Spain.

In the days when the Marequis lived in Paris, "La Belle Époque," the city must have been the most enchanting in the world. For the rest of his life, my father remembered it with real pleasure, and kept a vivid memory of the friendship that existed between him and his friend and master, Julián Gómez R.

On his return to Madrid in 1914, my father started working in José Ramírez I's workshop at 2 Concepción Jerónima Street (the firm remained at this same address until 1995).

He began by varnishing guitars, bandurias, and lutes which, as one could imagine, were built in the most traditional manner. This was done in the workshop, in an area no bigger than 25 square meters, in which there were three benches for the guitar makers and a little table near the balcony for the one varnishing. (In the photo on page 85, we can see the handyman Antonio Gómez standing by the bench, and my father, seated and varnishing).

The tools—planes, jack planes made of hard holm oak, chisels, and templates—were all very simple. The utensils were sharpened on a huge water stone, which was operated by a pedal. (More details of these procedures later.)

At this workshop, several dozens of instruments were constructed. Since constructing them took a long time, and varnishing came after this time, there would come a time when the varnisher would become unemployed and be without pay. Those were the damned days of class and rights fights. One worked ten hours a day and six days a week. Guitar sales were seasonal: from the end of the crop harvest until after Christmas. During the rest of the year, the master had great difficulty in maintaining his family and the workshop, paying his workmen's salaries, and paying for the storage of the instruments. In this context, Jose Ramírez I had more lean days than bonanzas. According to my father, he was a good master, a good person, and was honest with his employees.

My father, Manuel Rodriguez
Perez; born 1887, died 1958.
Photo taken in Paris some years
before World War I.

Jose Ramírez died in 1923. Until Jose Ramírez II replaced him in 1925, the handymen Alfonso Benito and Antonio Gómez managed the workshop. My father continued with his varnishing job.

Jose Ramírez II came to own the business at the age of 40. As Prat expresses in his luthier dictionary, "The American atmosphere in which he had lived made him into a useful and practical man." That was the difference between Jose Ramírez I and Jose Ramírez II. The former was a veritable maestro and a good businessman; the latter, although he had grown up in his father's workshop and had became a guitarist at the age of 20, simply brought together good handymen (M. Ramírez, García), then left for America and returned at the age of 40 without having ever touched a tool. Let logic reign! A luthier? A guitar maker?

My father continued working with Ramírez II until 1930, when he was dismissed upon the arrival of a varnisher from Valencia who charged less for his services. "He was a useful and practical man."

After this experience, my father continued varnishing guitars with other luthiers (Santos, Borreguero, Saturnino Rojas), and occasionally would varnish an instrument or two upon direct orders from clients. He never, ever varnished guitars for the other eminent luthier of the time, Domingo Esteso. That was Mrs. Esteso's job.

In 1925, my father married my dear mother, Asunción Fernández, who was born in Madrid in 1900. She was an ideal wife. With her fighting spirit, she was always at my father's side and an exemplary mother. May God keep her soul.

I was born in 1926, and my sister in 1928. The poverty experienced in those years by my family and by the rest of Spain makes our generation, in my opinion, the most productive and progressive that humanity has ever known.

In 1936, I was ten years old and about to start secondary school. The war was raging, and Madrid suffered from continuous bombardment by the pro-Franco aviation. At school, we were told that we were to be evacuated to Valencia, where the fighting had not as yet reached.

My sister and I, together with 50 other children from my neighborhood and from the school in Olmo Street, left for Valencia. When we got there, my sister and I were sent to different homes but I refused because my mother had asked me not to become separated from my sister. The plan to send us to different homes did not work. Shortly afterwards, we were all put together in a school.

My parents stayed in Madrid, with heavy hearts. Since my father was too old to go to war, he was not called up. They took their belongings, closed our flat in Ministriles Street, and came to pick us up at Picaña, where we were being taken care of.

There were 50 children living in a beautiful, large house, which had lots of rooms and was surrounded by orange and lemon trees. The oldest was ten years old and the youngest six. It was one of those properties which were taken over during the Civil War by Republican militiamen who served as "ornaments" to the Civil War: the Republicans, the Socialists, the Anarchists of the FAI, and the Trade Unions. In short, the misfits.

My parents arrived, spoke to the teacher who had taken wonderful care of us, and picked us up. My mother requested a room from the Picaña Town Council, and we lived there as refugees. We were allocated a room in an abandoned orange warehouse where there were other Spanish refugees.

My father, Manuel Rodriguez Perez, at 69. Photo taken by Ted Norman in 1956.

The war ended in March 1939. When we arrived at our flat in Ministriles Street, Marcelo Barbero had not yet left the front. He arrived days later after a long walk, in abject poverty, with misery on his back. We should not forget that he fought with the losers, the Republic. When Ramírez II learned that we had returned, he called Marcelo and my father and once again set up the Ramírez workshop—pioneer of the guitar profession of today.

The workshop was set up with Alfonso Benito, first handyman since Ramírez I; Marcelo Barbero, second handyman; my father, Manuel Rodriguez, varnisher; and I as a 13-year-old apprentice. The workshop had been formed by the same people as in 1925, with the exception of Antonio Gómez, who had died in the war, and myself, who was now starting out in this profession.

I worked as an apprentice for a year. As was usual in that post-war period, I came down with a fever that lasted for several weeks and did not allow me to work. My mother inherited some pesetas from my poor grandmother, and my father did some odd jobs as a "newsboy" for the *Ya* daily newspaper.

Because I was not allowed to work until I was 14, I went back to school to continue my studies. But even while I was studying, I continued as an apprentice, since Marcelo and my father did some odd jobs in their spare time and I would give them a hand.

But the money from the inheritance did not last long, and I soon had to go back to work. That was in 1941. I asked my father what kind of job I could do, and he advised me to look for another profession. We searched. I tried to study so as to get into the banking sector, but the schools were expensive, and my father's salary too low. The months went by, and one day, without telling my father anything, I presented myself at the Ramírez workshop. I offered my services as an apprentice and was accepted. The Ramírezes, who were somewhat idealistic and conservative—even to the point of having some feudal reminis-

My father, Manuel Rodriguez, in the Ramirez Workshop balcony, at 2 Conception Jeronim street, in the '20s.

cence—liked to have their workers' children follow their fathers' footsteps by working in their workshop. They loved to be depended upon.

My starting wage was five pesetas—a little more than in 1939 when I was given 1.50. I started by making all the inner parts of the bandurria, lute, and guitar—such as the sticks, bracings, and carving (thickening the wood). First these parts were made for the bandurrias and lutes, and later for the guitars—the last stage in apprenticeship.

The most arduous job was thickening the wood. We would spend several weeks doing it with fine-toothed planes and blades. It was hard work; some of those instruments, constructed with mahogany, bubinga, coral, and cypress, were disproportionately thick.

But that was the way to learn the trade. I remember with delight my relationship—not my salary—with the two Ramírez brothers, Pepe and Alfredo. We shared our hopes, our friendship; we talked about our love affairs, discussed politics and made future plans for our lives. We made plans for the guitar factory the Ramírezes were supposed to set up in Madrid, as well as the great crafts workshop. We even went hunting for potential premises. But destiny had other plans. The premature death of Alfredo Ramírez, when he was only 28 and newly married to his adorable wife, dashed our plans and changed our futures. His death was a very painful loss to me. He was an unforgettable gentleman. He died on 4 March 1954. I still have his keepsake.

A few months after starting work at Ramírez's, I set up my own working bench in my house at Ministriles Street. There I worked at little repair jobs given by my serenader friends, and other jobs that Marcelo, who lived in the flat above me, entrusted me with.

Thanks to the fraternity between the two families, I was able to start making my first guitars, bandurrias, and lutes. That was in 1944. We also made a lot of capos at home for flamenco guitars. Ramírez gave them to me to make at home and to keep me busy, so that I would not have time to do other jobs and be his competitor. It was a natural thing to do.

These capos were sold to the public at five pesetas. Ramírez paid me 2.50 pesetas for my workmanship and he kept the remaining 2.50. He also provided the leftover wood that could not serve any other purpose. Those were the days when Marcelo started working at the González workshop on Carretas Street, doing all the jobs they requested, and some of which I did.

Working at home, late at night and after a hard day's work at the workshop, is something that has been done by all those who belong to this profession. This was the way to get known publicly. And step by step, one would move up so that the professionals would take notice of our existence.

In those days, the majority of those in the guitar-making profession made flamenco guitars. All low-class young people dreamed of becoming artists, and what was in vogue was flamenco and traditional Spanish music. There were great folklore companies with prestigious artists from the singing, dancing, and flamenco groups that travelled around the world, and thanks to whom our art spread far and wide.

Back then, there was a great demand for dancers and guitarists, unlike the lack of demand for them today, which can be attributed to the high costs and lack of such artistic figures. Under the circumstances, the top artists gave lessons to the young people. As a result, guitar sales, especially flamenco, soared to a peak unheard of in history. Added to this was the fact that in those days, there were only a few guitar makers (Ramírez, Esteso, Barbero, and myself). That was in 1945.

My first guitar, signed and labeled by me, was a flamenco guitar that and I sold for 500 pesetas. With that money, I also bought my first tailor-made suit. I was 19 years old.

I was beginning to be known, which was quite an accomplishment when you consider that my father never worked for himself, but rather made instruments for other people in their workshops, and therefore never got to put his name on his work.

In those years, everything was scarce: wood, varnish; shellac was synthetic, and spirits were of low alcohol content. (Today, I would give that stuff to those shellac lovers, a ridiculous varnish for our days!) My poor father had a heck of a time varnishing a guitar.

Ramírez III was beginning to make his exquisite concert guitars. The family was always lucky in times of hardship. It was the late 1940s, and in Europe, people were still going through the painful post-war era.

Germany, the nation that had always supplied the industry with violin and guitar materials and accessories, had not yet recovered from the disasters of the war. It was therefore not even easy to obtain certain second-rate woods. One could, however, obtain some pinewood tops, courtesy of the guitar factories in Valencia. Bubinga and vermilion were used for the backs and sides, and samanguila for the necks. All these types of wood were brought in from Guinea. For the fingerboards, we used the hardest wood we could lay our hands on.

Coming back to the good luck that followed some people, I recall one day in the 1940s, as we were working in the Ramírez workshop on Concepción Jerónima Street, the lights went off in the flat above the shop. Switching off the lights was the signal used by those working in the shop to call those in the workshop; and surely enough, the maestro, José Ramírez II, called out our

In Madrid between 1946–1950. Thos who were working at the J. Ramirez Workshop, at 2 Conception Jeronima Street. L to R:

1.) Miguel Robles, a guitar builder from Granada, who made only bandurias and lutes. He was an unstable man.

2.) Back, Ramon Peñalver (Monchi). He spent all his life at the J. Ramirez Workshop. He did not make anything other than bandurias and lutes. He was a little brother to me. I knew him from birth and we grew up together at 6 Ministriles Street.

3.) Alfonso Benito, a real master guitar at the Ramirez's until the '50s.

4.) Me… with a lot of hair and in my 20s.

5.) My father, the workshop at the Benavente plaza in Madrid.

names: "Pepe, Manolo, come down!" And so we did; we went down. "Unload this cart in the street and take the wood up to the workshop." In actual fact, it was a cargo taxi—a motorized cart that could be rented on any square in Madrid. Pepe, Monchi, and I set to work. Monchi, or Ramón Peñalver, was quite a character himself. He was born eight days after I was, on Ministriles Street in the flat facing that of my family's. He started working, as a child, at Ramírez's a few years after I had, and he must have worked with them until he died in the mid-80s. My poor friend never got around to making guitars; he only made medium-priced bandurrias and lutes, which serves to confirm that some amount of natural talent is required to become a guitar maker.

Well, we got to the motorized cart and started unloading the wooden boards. We could not believe our eyes: a wonderful spruce board, cut to the same thickness as a piano top, of an old color and fine grain with a width of not less than 24 cm. There was enough material to make at least several dozen guitars with wonderful tops; and the wood must have been at least 50 years old.

Among the remaining boards we found more wonderful surprises: matured rosewood from Río, cedar necks from Cuba, and more woods that I cannot recall. Obviously, our question to the maestro was where he had obtained all this wood. Don José answered me, saying: "Manolo, do you remember that friend of your father's and of Marcelo's, who was called Señor Manolo, and who lived in Vallecas? This wood was his. He has died, and a friend visited me and told me that they looked good for making guitars. He asked me whether I was interested. Can you imagine?" When I saw it, I was speechless. "So, Pepe, here you are, here is wood for your guitars," Ramírez told his son.

And with the wood, Ramírez III constructed wonderful guitars, which are a living testimony to his skilful craftsmanship and design.

But who was this Señor Manolo, the vegetarian? A jack-of-all-trades and master of none. An avowed bachelor who had a small income that allowed him to live comfortably. He must have bought these spectacular pieces of wood (I still delight in the memories of them) from some piano maker or other craftsman in Madrid in the 1920s. And he must have kept them like a treasure in the hope that one day he would, in his desire to be a guitar luthier, be able to use them. His dreams died with him, but Ramírez III enjoyed using them for his exclusive guitars. This delight made Marcelo Barbero blind with rage. This Mr. Manolo, a friend of Marcelo's and my father's, was a polite and affable man who introduced Marcelo to a vegetarian diet. How often did we not throw away fermented wheat in Marcelo's house—wheat which he was supposed to eat as part of his naturalist diet on the recommendations of this gentleman! The vegetarian (guitar-maker's apprentice in his imagination, maestro in his dreams), shared meals at my house as well as at Marcelo's. He was even a witness at the Barberos' wedding.

This gentleman caused great indignation in the Barbero family, and obviously in mine as well, since it turned out that, after having lived with us during those long years of economic precariousness and shortage of decent wood, he had kept and hidden this precious material that is used exclusively for the guitar, and is the dream of any guitar maker. Luthiers from the 1950s onward knew the frustration of wanting to make the ideal guitar, but having only have mediocre materials at their disposal.

By God's grace, in the early 1950s, there were travellers coming from Germany who would bring us wood, which somehow alleviated the hardship of the trade. I have pleasant memories of a German aficionado who lived in Barcelona: Juan Sonntag, an expert in the metal and chemical industry who would send us wonderful German pine tops and bring us veneer of the purest color you can imagine.

The years went by at the Ramírezes, and Ramírez II grew older. His sons took more and more control of the business. The Ramírez brothers were more idealistic in their concept of work. Great were our hopes and excitement for the guitar. Those were the days when we experimented, when we dreamt of the big factory project, of the quality handcrafted production, of the factory for making student guitars.

To come back to the 1940s, Marcelo went independent again, and Alfonso Benito continued as maestro at Ramírez's.

In those days, given the precarious work conditions, there was a dire need for extra income. Benito also constructed musical instruments after his day's work at Ramírez's. We all had to do extra jobs wherever we could. This is because in the '40s, Spain was suffering from both the effects of the World War and the aftermath of the Civil War. There was an acute shortage of everything. Food was rationed, and food trading was illegal.

At the time, cheap, study guitars were constructed for Ramírez by the Vicente Tatay company in Valencia. Tatay himself would send us the guitars by the dozens, wrapped in straw and packed in huge wooden cases. He would also send us packets of rice bundled in the straw. Until the advent of democracy in the 1970s, we all had to do more than one job.

Señor Benito, good handyman that he was, constructed wonderful instruments to which he signed his name and his Galileo Street address—behind Ramírez's back, as had Marcelo, myself, and many others. Today, those instruments are collectors' pieces. At Ramírez I's workshop, Benito was the contemporary of Julián Gómez R., Rafael Casana, Enrique García, and Antonio Viudes. Obviously, he was the youngest of the four. All these handymen emancipated themselves from Ramírez and created their own guitars in their own workshops, with a signature and an identity of their own.

Alfonso Benito never left Ramírez's. He worked there for 50 years or more, and he was the maestro of maestros. He worked with us, bench to bench, and was always willing to offer words of advice.

I met Maestro Segovia when he returned to Spain in the early 1950s. There was a renewed interest in playing a guitar built by a Spanish luthier, and the gentlemanly Andrés Segovia visited the few luthiers that existed at the time in Madrid: Ramírez, Esteso, and Marcelo Barbero.

For social reasons, Señor Andrés chose Ramírez. In those years, we had rid ourselves of routine and were constructing the best concert and flamenco guitars one could create in Madrid. There was some rivalry and competition between Marcelo Barbero and Esteso's nephews.

I can recall how, in those years, the Madrid guitar makers would receive visits from almost all the provincial luthiers: M. de la Chica and Miguel Rodríguez Beneyto (old and bony). The famous Mariano Cubas, who lived on Concepción Jerónima Street up the street from Ramírez's, brought his guitar. We all went to see this wonderfully constructed guitar. Señor Rodríguez Beneyto had a veneer-topped guitar, very well-calibrated and with a perfect sound, though somewhat metallic.

Those were the years in which we had many visits, and it was a time of discovery for many. At the time, Robert Bouchet, the art professor, came to see Marcelo Barbero. I remember that Marcelo was not in the workshop, and Robert Bouchet asked for him at the entrance. This gentleman did not speak much Spanish, and my father tried to fish out his long-forgotten French, but with little success.

We were also visited by Tenorio, a friend of my father's who came from Buenos Aires, and by Manuel Reyes, who was just starting out. They all came to Madrid to get to know the Madrid luthiers' craftsmanship better. In those years, Madrid was the capital of the guitar, and had the most prestigious guitar conservatory of the musical world. The teachers then were Regino Sainz de la Maza, Pedro Moreno, La Fuente, José Ibáñez, the Esquembre family, Áureo Herrero, etc. The Madrid staff drew the attention of many, who did not hesitate to come and learn how to play the guitar with them, and who, in turn became future prestigious teachers.

In 1955, I decided to set up my own workshop in my house on Ministriles Street. In 1957, I moved my workshop to Jesús y María Street. In those years, I sent my guitars to many countries (France, England, and USA). Through some University of California-Los Angeles professors and a lawyer friend of mine,

I was able to emigrate to the US. I arrived in Los Angeles in July 1959, soon after getting married.

My father, who retired in 1953, died in 1958, but had the pleasure of seeing me start out in my profession, and the satisfaction of knowing that my guitars were appreciated—judging from the orders that never ceased pouring in, for bigger and bigger quantities. By God's grace, I lived my childhood and my adolescence with my family. My father was not just my master—as a man and as a professional—but also my very good friend. We shared everything; we discussed and talked about every matter and all that we did, and we did the best we could. I hope to be able to repeat this experience by living it with my sons.

My life in Los Angeles was marvellous. I had orders waiting when I arrived, and even before I had access to my materials and tools, which were being shipped there. I established my workshop, first in the town center, in the most commercial and chic area of the city. I was visited by my guitarist friends who were already familiar with my work, and others who knew nothing about me. I received a lot of orders for guitars.

This first workshop was in the luthier shop at 10400 Willshire Boulevard, in West Los Angeles, the so-called Miracle Mile. This shop was part of a flat loaned to me by Mr. Brown (Brown's Violin Shop), a subsidiary of the Whilezer collection and representative in Los Angeles. Mr. Brown was a guarantor for my entry to the USA; and thanks to the arrangements of my dear friend, Arthur E. Macbeth, an eminent lawyer, we entered with a preferential visa.

Mr. Brown was already elderly and infirm, so his wife ran the shop. We did not stay there long, since there was not enough room to hang my guitars and, what is more, they were interior premises. And yet the love and gratitude I feel for Mr. Brown and his family is so deep, as they helped launch my career when we arrived. In his establishment, I enjoyed his wisdom and knowledge on violins—glorious violins that I was able to hold in my hands. The feel of a Stradivarius or an Amati is beyond words. I was introduced to distinguished violinists and cellists who visited the shop, and who are now considered immortal talents of those instruments.

My second workshop was at 1010 North Highland Avenue in Hollywood, three blocks north of Hollywood Boulevard. It was also a half a kilometer to the south of the famous Hollywood World and the entrance to the Ventura Freeway, the usual route to San Fernando Valley and the cinema studios. Many artists and musicians of the cinema industry visited us at that house. Those were the years in which my popularity was at its highest point.

From the summer of 1959 until April 1973, when I closed down my workshop to return to Madrid, I seldom had the chance to display a guitar constructed by me for more than two months—the necessary waiting period before the buyer usually came for it. In the United States, I always worked on request and with advance orders. I constructed guitars for many different people, from cinema professionals in Hollywood to retired people who, in their long-awaited free time, felt the need to express themselves through music. Hollywood was the capital of cinema and music. Many of the great maestros of this century lived and worked at their art in this city. Most of them spent their days in the film sound studios, and some of them played the classical guitar.

A few months later, my workshop and my relationship with the Los Angeles teachers became consolidated. Flamenco was also in fashion in those years, and the last flamenco companies were enjoying great success in the US. In the meantime, I was building guitar after guitar, and I must have been charging three times more than my colleagues in Spain were charging.

At that time, I was visited by a wonderful composer, guitarist, first violinist of the Los Angeles Symphony, and a friend of Andrés Segovia and Stravinsky: Theodore Norman. He asked me how we could improve the tuning of the guitar. Until then, there had been much talk on the subject, but little had been done. The difficulty arose from the fact that the frets on the fingerboard are fixed points. All my colleagues before me had worked according to the "Aguado law," which stated that the first fret had to be equal to 1/18 the distance of the bridge to the nut. This is how my movable bridge was born, as I shall explain further on.

But time went by, and one day, without any warning, we were informed that our building was going to be torn down. So, we moved to our own house at 8410 West Third Street, Los Angeles. In 1963 my first son, Manuel Jr. was born. My wife—my partner, the fondest admirer of my guitars, and by this time, my precious collaborator—was also my best critic. Her experience makes her judgement a necessary part of my work. Moreover, she paints with great taste and talent, and her work arouses the admiration of our artist friends. Our son Norman was born in 1965. In those years, Maestro Segovia saw my guitars and, together with his wife, Doña Emilia (whom I met when she was a young girl with her father, Señor E. Corral), encouraged me in my work. I sent to him, while he was in New York, one of my guitars with my moveable bridge; and Segovia was photographed playing it. Later on, the picture was published in his book *Segovia Technique*. Page 32 of that book has a picture of the maestro showing the position to play the classical guitar on an instrument whose head and movable bridge I constructed.

Andrés Segovia gave this guitar, which I hope is still giving pleasure, to his disciple and friend Señor Silva, a professor from a university on the the East Coast of United States.

Years later, I sent him another guitar through my brothers, and he has kept it to this day. It was given to him in Madrid, and the maestro, who was such a nice gentleman, wrote me a letter from Munich, acknowledging its receipt.

In 1973, I paid him a visit in Madrid, and he told me that he still had the guitar, but that he planned to exchange it for a better one I would make in the future. But how can a guitar-making craftsman have a series of guitars at any given time for him to choose the one he liked best? My guitar production is very personal, and therefore very limited. It allows me to have good financial independence, but not enough to allow me to have half a dozen guitars on display for people to choose from. For this reason, the maestro tried guitars constructed by the many luthiers of the guitar family. In these past years, he has mainly used the services of a constructor with a workforce of 20 people.

Years went by, and our children's childhood years were a delightful time for us. We lived our golden years near dear friends in the USA. In the 1960s, the Japanese boom began. My workshop was at 8410 West Third Street, one street away from La Ciénaga, which one only had to cross to get to Beverly Hills. We had our shop and workshop on the ground floor of this building, and our flat on the floor above. There could not have been a better location, since this provided direct and easy access to the freeways.

I became acquainted with the Japanese industry through the wife of my friend, Mr. R. Mann: a publicist who offered me, at a bargain price, the first Toyota car model to be put on show at his car dealer's shop. It was very similar to the Seat of those years. I imagine that today it would be a collectors' model. Those were the John F. Kennedy years in the USA.

Japan was beginning to make reproductions of all kinds of already-invented articles and anything else imaginable, including our guitar. At that time, the guitars on the American market came from Sweden: the "España" and the "Goya," typical German construction guitars, each which had the neck fitted into the box, following the model of bowed stringed instruments. Guitars from Mexico also found their way into California. Those were the cheapest, since, in that country, everybody constructed guitars—from the mayor to the altar boy. The best quality ones were those by Pimentel and Solís.

However, Americans did not go crazy over the Valencian guitars, and they flopped. Moreover, for Valencian guitars to be known, one needed time to go around paying visits and showing them, and I simply did not have the time.

Even so, given the demand, some business-minded wholesalers sent some unidentified guitars to Japan for reproduction. The first of these did not meet the minimum requirements, but were the cheapest ($25 and 35) for the general public. Just imagine what the factory price would have been.

Naturally, the Japanese, always are always so skillful, saw that the demand for their guitars was high, and obtained models of guitars from prestigious makers and faithfully copied them for a good price. The outcome? They invaded the guitar market. At the same time, they became interested in guitar making and came to Spain to learn. For a few measly pesetas, and out of vanity, some luthiers sold our art and our tradition.

I recall that the sales agency that represented the most prestigious piano and guitar firm, as well as other instrument makers, had no idea whatsoever of what a guitar was. These gentlemen called to ask me if I could show them the basic components of a guitar. They came to visit, and I simply explained it to them. Today, this firm is still making guitars. Personally, I have had various requests from Japanese companies who were willing to pay me very handsomely to teach them. I have always declined. My knowledge and skill belong to my children and my school, and my tradition belongs to the maestros who preceded me.

I am pleased to acknowledge that the Japanese industry has done a good job in the construction of our classical guitar. By spreading their trade around the world, they managed to get many guitarists excited about our guitar. Moreover, Japan enjoyed the guitar through the creation of music academies and institutions, which have large numbers of students under the guidance of distinguished professors. Today, many of these students are concert artists themselves.

For economic reasons, Spain today is no longer the great manufacturer of bargain goods for so many industries. Now it is other countries that have opened factories with cheap labor and are producing their merchandise for the whole world. Included in those items are guitars of traditional Japanese firms made in Korea and Ceylon.

As a result of the price competition provoked by the Japanese guitar, many people simply bought industrially produced instruments, since the handcrafted guitars cost twice as much. Obviously, such buyers were not aware of these guitars' true value—a $400 guitar was acquired by the retailer at half that price, the wholesaler earned 40% with transport and tax, and thus the real value of the instrument was not more than $100. However, the luthier's guitar is much more expensive, owing to the high-quality woods, the personal dedication of the artists, and the time consumed in its construction. I must say, that when all is said and done, an industrially made, imitation handcrafted guitar can be just as worthy and meet the taste of the guitarist.

In 1973, I returned to Madrid and opened my workshop on Hortaleza Street, where it is still located today. My sons were at an ideal age to make the move: Manuel was 11, Norman 8, and I, at 46, still had enough strength to start all over again. *From Madrid, my guitars are for the rest of the world.* This was the idea that spurred us to return to Madrid, even though I love the States, and I shall love it as long as I live.

We came back and my orders, by God's grace, did not shrink. The Japanese guitar boom also manifested itself in the demand for quality Spanish guitars. The Niibori Academy and many other importers placed large numbers of orders for our guitars.

In that period, Madrid was brewing with guitarists from all over the world who were learning at the Conservatory. These students, who are today teachers in their places of origin, studied in Madrid for the required number of years; and upon returning to their respective countries, would obtain professorships in the conservatories of the cities in which they lived.

Naturally, orders from Europe multiplied; not to mention those from the USA and Japan. Our lives became comfortable and quietly routine, but I sorely missed my home and my friends in Los Angeles.

The Spanish quality guitar sector was held in high esteem, and demand was high. All the craftsmen of Madrid were in high demand. In the late 1960s, more luthiers arose, following the Madrid school, and making names for themselves all over the world. In the meantime, my sons were studying and growing up, until the time came for them to decide what their profession would be. Logically, Manuel was the first to take that step, and he decided to follow my footsteps and make guitars with me. In 1978, he began his career as a guitar maker and, in 1982, he came with us to the guitar craftsmen exhibition in Frankfurt.

We therefore participated in the World Musical Fair in Frankfurt (as well as that of Anaheim, in the USA) where the most magnificent instruments were exhibited.

I must say, sincerely, that owing to their ignorance of what a musical instrument consists of, most people do not fully appreciate music. That great sound-producing machine, the orchestra, has life because each and every one of the instruments that make it up is a sophisticated precision tool made to produce the sound that corresponds to it, and which has been chosen by the director and composer of the score. So, this is what a fair is all about: serving as a showcase for its industry, providing potential business for the tradesmen, and giving curious visitors a chance to know every bit about a musical instrument.

At the fair, we rented a medium-sized stand, and each one of us eight luthiers exhibited our guitars, (as can be seen in the photographs on pages 64–65), without any rivalry. The comparisons of, and thus the differences between our guitars, is the fruit of our diversity and our virtue. And it is precisely in this diversity that our know-how is portrayed in the artistic world.

It was a splendid fair for the guitar industry. All kinds of people visited us: fellow craftsmen from other countries, manufacturers, wholesalers, traders, and guitarists from all over the world. For all eight of us, it was an unforgettable experience; for some, the first exhibition outside of Spain and an opportunity to make oneself known.

On my own initiative, I visited the stand exhibiting guitars from the veteran firm of the Madrid school. As we knew each other, I kindly invited the representative who manned the stand to visit our stand, and asked if he would like to have a picture taken with us. He gruffly refused to do so. That was a shame, because Madrid guitar history would have boasted of an important photographic record which I personally would have cherished. Sometimes, vanity inescapably obstructs history.

For instance, here is this wonderful picture of Manuel Ramírez's workshop with his handymen at the door, which appeared in many publications.

1.4 Our Workshop: Manuel Jr. and Myself

1983 marked the beginning of a new phase in the Rodríguez tour. After our trip to Frankfurt, my son Manuel simply was not satisfied with just waiting for his guitars to be displayed in the shop until they got sold. At 20, he was already entrepreneurial, a trait that has always characterized him. Not only did he work with me in the workshop, but he also afforded himself little luxuries by doing extra work, such as teaching English classes in a number of public schools and language schools. With his earnings, he bought himself his first car, a used Seat 133. He continued working hard, and with his income from teaching and the sale of his guitars, he was able to buy his first brand new car, a Renault 11. Months later, he travelled to London with one of our guitars, which he had constructed himself, and visited the leading guitar spots: guitar shops, academies, and the guitarists themselves. He managed to get articles written in *Classic Guitar Magazine* and in *Magazine Guitar International*.

He returned to Madrid with the hope that those who saw his guitar would demand its production. He sold some, but not all. The following summer, in 1984, he returned to England with his flashy Renault 11 and his guitars—quality ones and medium-priced, sturdy ones constructed by certain manufacturers who were already supplying us with guitars for sale in the Hortaleza Street shop. These guitars were created in a special way, which allowed me to stick in a label with our name that read "Constructed for..."

One day, Manuel called me from London and told me that he had orders for these medium-priced guitars, and that it would be interesting to have a range of guitars priced from medium to high—in addition to the handmade ones. We became somewhat inspired and decided to create our own wholesale commercial line of handcrafted guitars. To achieve this, we decided to visit all the music shops in Europe: in France, England, Belgium, Netherlands, Luxembourg, Germany, Switzerland, and France. This trip kept us on the road for three months. We did not think that bringing a few guitars would be enough to catch the attention and earn the trust of all the shops we were visiting, so we decided to take all our different models of guitars for each client to see, try, select, and buy on the spot. We therefore bought a 5-ton Mercedes lorry (see photos, page 63), which could store 500 guitars. My son Manuel had to get a lorry driver's license very quickly so that we could take to the highways.

The guitars we took along were made to our specifications by three trustworthy manufacturers. I made a catalogue with pictures, and my wife Emilia designed a collage for the cover.

In the spring of 1984, we began our trip in Madrid and passed through Zaagoza, Barcelona, and La Junquera (the Spanish side of the French border).

Our Shop, Madrid, 1983

Spain was not yet a member of the EEC (European Economics Community). "God protects the ignorant," because when we arrived at the French border, we had to obtain a number of permits, licenses, and make advance payments for official documentation fees through a payment office. At the Spanish border, La Junquera was packed with lorries leaving or entering the country. To request export permits, we had to use intermediaries who had their contact offices in France on the other side of the border. After long waits—in some cases after spending the night at a hotel—we would finally obtain the permit. We would then get back on the road and drive towards Le Bolue, get into the French customs area, and start all over again—handing over documents, bills, requesting an import permit (for France), and a circulation permit for the French territory.

One has to admit that France has been forced into being a transit country for all kinds of vehicles: from cargo to private and passenger vehicles, not forgetting buses, and lorries. You cannot imagine what one could take, bring, and leave in all these incoming and outgoing movements. That is why France had so many customs officers stationed all over the country. These kind-hearted officers felt some amount of disbelief as they saw us arrive in our flashy lorry loaded with our guitars and posted with advertisements. They would often stop us and request to see our documentation. On a number of occasions, they made us open the lorry for their dogs to sniff for drugs. On one occasion, I remember them taking us to a police station where they made us unload each and every one of the guitars for their inspection, one by one. Since we had nothing to hide, the following day found us back on the road again.

After crossing France, we knocked at the doors of every music shop, offering and selling our guitars all along the way to England, towards Dover and the English Channel.

We would start off at Montpellier. Whenever we reached a new city we would get the Yellow Pages and telephone directories and find the names and addresses of the music houses. We then went to Nîmes, Valence, and Lyon before we got to Paris, and continued from there to Lille and Calais. In the latter, with our lorry a little emptier, we took the ferry that would take us to Dover.

Our trips across French territory, most especially the first ones, were simply fantastic. It was no easy feat crossing it, due to our inability to speak French. In the music establishments we visited, the people were polite, but did not speak either Spanish or English.

That is why getting to Dover meant some sort of relaxation. Being able to understand the other's language made our business easier, in spite of having

Manuel and myself

to drive on the left—a task which imposed no hardship for Manuel. When we left Dover, after having made the necessary customs payments, we drove towards London, where we had friends such as Ivor Mairants and his wife Lily, whom we got to know in 1955 and who visited us in Los Angeles. We also left guitars at the Ivor Mairants Musicentre.

As we continued on our journey, we arrived at Bristol, where we met Michael Watson; and from Bristol we drove on to Oxford, Cheltenham, Birmingham, Newcastle upon Tyne, Manchester, Bradford, Leeds, Sheffield, Nottingham, Leicester, Northampton and back again to Dover.

Wholesale Lorry

Once we got back to France, we headed for Brussels, Bruges, and Antwerp; and as usual, our lorry provided us with those joys that are only known to the traveller. Visiting Europe and crossing its territory is a joy that allows one to forget about all the work and effort involved in being away from home for three months.

In the Netherlands, there are extraordinary highways and roads, and it was therefore not difficult at all to get to the smallest towns, although they were more densely populated, as if it were a question of stretching out one's arm and touching beautiful lakes. There was Eindhoven, Breda, The Hague, Amsterdam, and Groningen, after crossing the dyke from Alkmaar. This is how we reached Germany and visited Bremen, Hamburg, Lübeck, Hannover, Cologne, Koblenz, and Frankfurt until we got to Switzerland through Basel, Zürich, Liechtenstein, Lucerne, Lausanne, Geneva, and finally Mulhouse.

Germany and Switzerland are full of little villages, lakes, mountains, and quaint historical city quarters. Driving through these streets, stopping at red traffic lights, and gazing at it all, even if from the other side of a windscreen, is a privilege. And most of all, the people we met. Obliging and interested in our guitars, they would buy and place orders, and even those we could not convince would at least receive us politely and very respectfully.

So as a result of our trips and efforts, we have managed to gain credibility in our service and high esteem for the quality of our guitars in both Europe and the United States. With our samples, we have travelled across the greater part of the Eastern USA, including Chicago and Boston.

In 1986, my son Manuel travelled to his hometown in California, meeting new people and making friends while showing our models. He would later receive orders from them. For the first time, we attended and exhibited at the wonderful Anaheim Fair. It was such a great pleasure to take part in this fair, to hug my friends and have meals with them. I remember that we visited our former house at 8410 West Third Street. Today, these visits to Los Angeles constitute an unmissable event that allow us to enjoy the city in which I lived for 14 years. For the Rodríguez family, it is an honor and a pleasure to be a part of the Fender family, who are currently distributors of our guitars.

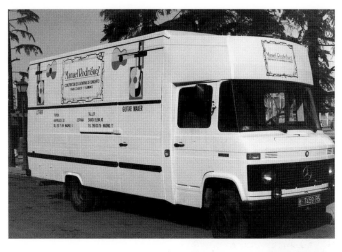

Between 1987 and 1989, we were already known in Europe. We travelled there once a year, and made telephone sales with constant and carefully given service. The common market and the opening of foreign borders accorded us freer movement. We were therefore able to send our guitars straight to the shops, thanks to the contact list my sons and I created on our trips with the lorry—progress made while on the move. But at that time, we saw the need to have wholesale representatives who would distribute our products in each country. And we found them. Wholesalers from different places agreed to represent us, and with great interest. Given that there is a high demand for guitars bearing our name, we are ethically obliged to construct instruments with the personality and identity of our brand, which is not an easy task at all. Things are not perfect when the instructions to make them are dictated. The only guitar that is really your guitar is the one created through your own experience. After 50 years in the trade, I believe that the trademark owner must create the guitar that he offers and sells to his clients as an instrument on which he can confidently put his name, his signature, and his personal guarantee.

Five-ton Mercedes lorry that held 500 guitars on our European tour.

In June 1994, after displaying our guitars in our shop at 26 Hortaleza Street, my wife Emilia and I decided to create our own guitar factory so as to put into practice the principle that has governed our business. Our prestige and our duty to our clients obliged us to construct each instrument in a personal manner.

Thanks to an inheritance from Emilia's parents, we were able to mobilize the necessary financial resources to make the project a reality. In August of that same year, we rented the premises in which we would subsequently set up the genuine Manuel Rodríguez and Sons Guitar Factory. It is located on the outskirts of the town of Illescas, in the province of Toledo, close to Madrid. After shopping around, we chose this building (see photos, page 64), and took over the three floors into which it is divided. On the ground floor we set up the sawing room where we placed the machines used for constructing guitar parts, as well as the oven in which the wood is dried. On the left is the warehouse and the place where guitars are strung. On the second floor we set up the production room, where the sanding and polishing are done, and the depressurised chamber for varnishing is located. The third floor is a wonderful climatized room for our guitars where, after drying in the chamber, they are dried to completion in natural heat and air.

Illescas (1995–1999)

Today. Esquivias – Toledo.

This is how the original renditions of our guitars were born, following the experience that was accumulated over the years and over a long professional life. Today, our guitars, which are authentic models we ourselves have designed, are present in the EU, with the guarantee of the trust placed in us and of our prestige.

As a family-run company, each one of us has a specific task to perform. As at the beginning of our marriage, my wife ran the shop, just as she did in Los Angeles and at 32 Hortaleza Street, Madrid. At present, she is a well-qualified guitar and accessories saleswoman at our sales point at 26 Hortaleza.

Our son Norman is taking over the running of the shop, learning from his mother's experience. Manuel and I are fully dedicated to the factory-handcraft workshop at Esquivias, where we have the joy of constructing guitars and the zeal for achieving optimum quality, which we share with our workforce. Manuel is the manager of the factory, the wood purchasing officer, the personnel manager, the sales manager, the accountant, the quality inspector and the one in charge of ordering any guitar consignments out of the factory. In the guitar manufacturing process, I, Manuel Rodríguez Sr., am in charge of quality development and play the role of the spiritual leader of the company, as befits my age. And as long as my sensorial capacities do not fail me, I will continue to construct my guitars personally, with the guarantee that the one that I sign is created by me, with my own hands, wholeheartedly.

Our fairs and stands

Frankfurt; our stands, 1986.

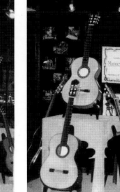

Frankfurt fair

Frankfurt fair

Anaheim fair with Fender.

Anaheim fair

Anaheim fair with Fender: Jim Cruckshank, me, Ed Rizzuto, William Schultz.

Taiwan fair

Chapter 2

*Guitars: The Woods Used
and Their Origin in the World.
Wood Maps and Pictures.*

*Suena guitarra, suena… tu voz levanta:
Contigo un pueblo entero suspira y canta.
Donde un enamorado viva dichoso
Donde exista una moza y haya una reja,
allí habrá una guitarra seguramente
y donde estén sus notas y su alegría
allí está el alma entera de Andalucía*

B. FLORES

2.1. The Guitar and Its Wood

Both the playing of classical music in its strictest, orthodox form of musical composition, and of any of the other diverse styles, necessitates the need for perfection in a musical instrument. A sound volume and quality that is mild and affable, and a clearly distinct intonation are the minimum requirements for a musical instrument. But in our guitar, as in all music-making instruments made of wood, the aim is also to attain perfection in its construction.

Therefore, the art of knowing and working with Mother Nature's wood is one of the noblest occupations created for the development and enjoyment of human beings. Knowing the qualities of weight, hardness, elasticity, and resistance of wood and the diverse varieties of ecological systems in which it grows and develops on this planet are vital. For centuries, wood from all different continents have been used in the construction of the guitar.

Spruce

This wood grows, in its different varieties, all over Europe, except in Denmark, the Netherlands and Western Russia. The optimum trees with which to construct instruments thrive on the high mountains of Central Europe: Germany, Romania, the former Czechoslovakia, and the cold countries. The most unsuitable trees for our guitars are those obtained from the south and the coastal areas, for the simple reason that their development is faster and their grain is broader and knottier.

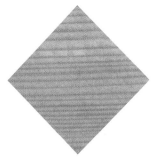

Picea abies
Family: Pinaceae
SPRUCE, EUROPEAN or
WHITEWOOD (S)

These trees are magnificent in size, height, straightness, and slenderness. They can grow to a height of 36.6 meters and a diameter of 0.76 to 1.2 meters. In the Romanian mountains, they can grow up to 61 meters high, with a diameter of between 1.5 and 1.8 meters. The wood is white in color, changing to golden-yellow on drying. Their annual growth is clearly defined in the rings of the grain that are straight and beautiful in texture. This wood's weight, after a certain time and maturing, is 470 kg/m. The transmission speed of sound waves through the grain of the pine reaches 3,320 meters per second, versus that of maple acer, which is 4,111 meters per second, and that of steel, which is around 5,000 meters per second (calculations taken from musical acoustics).

The nature and transmission of sound are, therefore, the elements that reveal the magnificent nature of the material; by which, and with observation and intuition, luthier shave conceived this family of bowed stringed instruments.

Played with a chin holder, without any interference or contact, these instruments, with the highest purity, send out their sound waves, transmitted through their pine and maple acer wood, via the soundboard and the back.

With a sustained stroking of the bow, they also produce the most perfect sounds, capable of reaching the utmost limits.

The density of pine, in comparison with ebony, is 1.2; rosewood 1 or 0.82; spruce 0.4; Western Red Cedar 0.3; Black Poplar 0.2. Dense woods such as ebony and rosewood, etc. shrink, have a strong and peculiar smell and, by their nature, take a longer time to dry. Pinewood, in a dry climate or surroundings, in the open air with a lot of light and sun, is suitable. With it, you can construct a perfect soundboard in a minimum drying time, ranging from 8 to 10 years. As a practical example, the ideal wood for a concert guitar is one from a tree felled in 1960 and used in 1990. Its guarantee, in sound and other qualities, is assured. The higher the humidity, the higher the density and the weight and the less the elasticity.

Matured wood—with more years—is less dense, stiffer, and has less weight, although its stiffness depends to a greater extent on its grain and the oxidization of the resin (the pine is very resinous). In this also lies its richness. From time immemorial, resin has been put to different uses: for waterproofing, varnishing, etc. I will deal with resin when I talk about my ideas on varnishes in later chapters.

Western Red Cedar

Since the beginning of the 1960s, we have been using this type of wood in substitution for the pine (*Picea abies*). In my Los Angeles years, I undertook a search for wood warehouses in that city. In the Penberthy import shop, which sold wood from all over the planet, I was sold some boards—perfectly cut out for our instruments. That wood was Western Red Cedar (*Thuja plicata*). It had been cut many years back and was very dry. Cedar has a central appearance that is all "whiteness," unlike its hard part, which becomes more or less dark chocolate brown. The part that gets darkened most is the dead part of the tree. It grows on the West Coasts of the USA and Canada; to be precise, it thrives in the British Columbia areas of Canada, from California to Alaska. It also grows in England and New Zealand. It reaches a height of 46 to 76 meters, and has a diameter of 90 cm to 2.5 meters. Its weight is 370 kg. It is special because, in small pieces, it dries out so quickly and, due to the fact that it hardly shrinks, does not break. However, with straight grain and clear growth design in its rings, it has neither the brightness nor the fine texture of the pine. Its sawdust, after sanding, is very fine and volatile—harmful to one's health. When inhaled, it may even affect the lungs in the long run.

Thuya plicata
Family: Cupressaceae
WESTERN RED CEDAR (S)

In the creation of guitar soundboards, once the wood is cut to the thickness and size needed, its drying is easier. Atmospheric changes hardly have any effects on it. In the past 30 years we have been working with this wood, and a respectable portion of my guitar production comes from this type of cedar.

My own personal impression is that this tree is similar to the pine. It is large in size, both height and diameter. It has slow growth in high and cold areas in northwest America, Canada and Alaska. Its grain and annual growth rings are exactly the same as those of Picea abies, which grows in the highlands of Central Europe. It even has the same stiffness.

When you compare the weight of the cedar (370 kg/m) with that of the pine (470 kg/m) you get a difference of 100 kg. This may well be one of the main reasons why cedar wood sounds more easily under similar conditions than the pine, because of its grain and stiffness.

One more curiosity. Looking at the world map, I see that both species, so different and yet so similar, grow on the same latitude, on the same parallel that crosses America and Europe. One of the causes of the disappearance of the pine is its use in guitar construction. Since the devastation of the European war (World War II) the enormous demand and consumption have forced European timber businessmen to fell large numbers of trees which have cost nature so many centuries to develop. Today, trees of the same species are being used to reforest Europe. May the heavens forbid us from having any other devastation that human malice can bring about, and may these young trees reach maturity so that our descendants can appreciate and enjoy all their magnificence.

Sequoia or Redwood. Bot. Sequoia sempervirens. Gravity = 0.37

The giant redwood, or sequoia, is is the oldest tree on the planet. The species grows in California, where the biggest trees you ever saw thrive. Its height can range from 61 to 104 meters. Strangely, its diameter is also between 61 to 104 centimeters. Its weight is 420 kg/m, and its growth is characterized by straight grain and rings with clear designs. It has a more reddish color than the cedar, but in other respects they both have similar characteristics. The sequoia weighs 50 kg more than the cedar and dries out easily. It is hardly flexible, easy to work on and has good finishing. Its texture is much like that of cardboard, and its weight does not provide very good sound results when compared with either the pine or the cedar. I still have very old sequoia wood but I rarely use it.

South American Cedar

This is the wood that we use for the neck of the guitar. The *cedro odorata* variety from Central America, Honduras, Nicaragua, and Mexico is the most valued one. This variety grows to a height of 21 to 30 meters and attains a diameter of 1 or 2 meters. Light or reddish brown in color, a fine texture, occasionally found with slow growth rings and straight grain, it has pleasant-smelling resin. The Spanish colonial settlers of old used it in making boxes to keep their clothes, as its smell served as an insect repellent. It is for this same reason that it is used for making cigar boxes. In the guitar industry, it is used on account of its light weight, which varies, depending on the species and the place of growth (between 370 and 750 kg/m; although the average is around 480 kg/m). When very dry, it is stable and has an average density. It is quite easy to work with, regardless of the fact that, on occasion, its grain follows different directions. Once varnished, it is of great beauty, and its grain magnifies its superb appearance.

Cedrela spp.
Family: Meliaceae
SOUTH AMERICAN CEDAR

Indian Rosewood

Another great tree of this glorious planet of ours, perhaps the most valued and magnificent is the Indian Rosewood. It grows in the south of India. Its height can reach 25 meters and its diameter ranges from 30 centimeters to 1.5 meters; the average being 80 cm. It forms a cylindrical trunk 6 to 15 meters high. It is also known as Bombay Rosewood, and in the UK, Bombay or Black Wood. Purple in color with a straight grain, it dries out easily. It is a great satisfaction to work with this wood, due to its texture and fragrance. Its weight, once dry, is 850 kg/m. Even though it dries easily, the ideal thing is to let it dry out slowly and in the open air, as this improves its color and stability. It is quite dense and easy to tame. It is of average stiffness and has a uniform texture. It has a good finish, especially once varnished, which gives it a remarkable appearance. It gives good results when used for guitar backs and sides. It responds magnificently in the transmission of good-quality sound of high volume. It is often said that this wood, like Brazilian Rosewood, has nothing to do with, nor contributes to, the sound of the guitar. However, as the soundboard vibration reveals, it is a well-known fact that some of the best guitars with great sound quality and volume were constructed with these two woods: the Indian and the Brazilian Rosewoods. It is also true that very many guitars have been created with backs and sides made from such woods as mahogany, walnut and maple, but there is no known top-quality guitar with its back or sides made from these latter woods.

Dalberfia latifolia
Family: Leguminosae
INDIAN ROSEWOOD

Dalberfia spp.
Family: Leguminosae
ROSEWOOD (BRAZILIAN and
HONDURAS)

Brazilian and Honduran Rosewood

This wood produces a mixture of diverse colors, such as brown, black, and violet; and in some cases, it even has grain that is red, green, and some parts that are greyish white. These colors, framed in a whimsical grain design, can create amazing abstract drawings that are fantastic in nature. Without any doubt at all, this is the most beautiful wood ever created by Nature. And our guitar-making industry, with the artistic spirit that this wood can evoke in us, is obliged to create a musical instrument into which we pour all our stylistic veins. With this wood, plus our taste in decorative craftsmanship, producing a work that gives satisfaction to the senses of hearing and sight is not such a difficult task. Thanks to its affable and steady sounds and very distinct intonation, the ear delights; and the combination of the wood's beauty and our taste in decoration let the eyes feast on its exquisiteness.

Brazilian Rosewood weighs 850 kg/m; Honduran Rosewood around 930 to 1,100 kg/m. Both take an awful lot of time to dry out, owing to the ease with which they break. They are very pleasant to work with, though difficult to cut to the grain. They are also very porous, and it is really difficult to cover the pores and obtain glossy varnishing that does not eclipse its colors and beauty.

There are a lot of differences between Honduran and Brazilian rosewoods. Honduras is 50% heavier and its grain has neither the color nor the beauty of Rio rosewood, the most beautiful one that grows in the inner forests of the humid jungle, among the most marvellous species in the world. Its aroma is sweet and pleasant.

East Indian Ebony. Bot. Diospyrus spp.
Ebenacede family. Gravity = 1.13

There are two kinds of ebony: the one that grows in India and the one that thrives in Africa. On account of its hardness and density, it is our ideal candidate for a durable, flat, and straight fingerboard.

Ceylon Ebony. Bot. D. Ebenum

Known as the true ebony, it is a hard wood, uniform in color and completely black. There are multitudes of species in different parts of India and Madagascar, such as Indian ebony, the famous Andaman marble wood from the Andaman Islands. All the species are small in size, with trunks measuring between 4.5 and 6 meters in height and from 30 to 60 centimeters in diameter. Apparently, the heart of Ceylonese ebony is completely black and its outer layer is greyer. Naga ebony is blackish-brown with beige grain and black stripes. The grain ranges from straight to irregular lines; when polished it may have a fine texture or metallic lustre.

Properties: the ebony of Ceylon weighs 1,190 kg/m. Indian ebony is a lot lighter, weighing 880 kg/m when dry. In general, ebony takes quite a few years to dry out and breaks easily if the cuts are not protected.

African Ebony

The heart of the trunk of the African Ebony is predominantly black. It grows in the south of Nigeria, Ghana, Cameroon, and Zaire, hence its name. Its height ranges between 15 and 18 meters, with an average diameter of 60 centimeters. From ancient Egyptian times it has been highly prized and in great demand.

It has an average weight of 1.30 kg/m when matured. It dries easily in the open, and once cut out into pieces, its transversal grain should be covered with thick paint or liquid wax in order to seal off all air passages and avoid fragmentation

This is one of the densest and hardest woods, and its color, all-around black, is of great beauty. When polished, it looks like a very clear mirror.

Diospyrus spp.
Family: Ebenaceae
AFRICAN EBONY

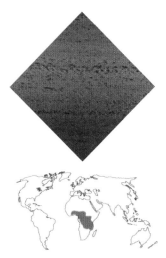

Entandrophragma cylindricum
Family: Meliaceae
SAPELE

Other Woods Used in Guitar-Making:
Sapele

This wood is used for our guitars in substitution for American Mahogany. Currently we used it for constructing necks, backs, and sides in student guitars. It is produced in Africa, in the western, central, and eastern tropical forests, from the Ivory Coast, Ghana, Nigeria, Cameroon, through to Uganda, Zaire, and Tanzania. Brownish salmon in color, with a close grain, it weighs between 560 and 690 kg/m, and can reach a height of 45 to 60 meters, with a diameter of 1 meter.

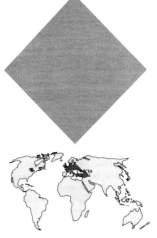

Acer pseudoplatanus
Family: Aceraceae
SYCAMORE

Sycamore

The Sycamore grows in Europe, the UK, and Western Asia. It reaches a height of 35 meters and has a diameter of 1.5 meters. Whitish cream in color, it dries slowly, with a straight grain which, on occasion, has beautiful waves.

Its medium-density wood weighs 610 kg/m, and is used for the construction of student guitars and student flamenco guitars, as much for its light color as for its density. Since it belongs to the acer family, it is a good transmitter of sound, and is therefore used in the construction of medium-quality violins.

Maple

This silver-colored wood is the ideal wood for bowed stringed instruments. Considering that we are talking about a wood that can transmit the highest levels of sound waves through its grain, it is the ideal choice for the most magnificent instruments ever created by man: the violin and its family.

This acer grows freely in certain parts of Europe, and there are over ten varieties of it in North America and Canada. It has a height of 30 to 40 meters and a diameter of between 60 and 120 centimeters. Depending on the species, its weight can range between 540 and 610 kg/m. It has a medium density, and once dry, which it becomes easily and slowly, it takes on a golden color. The most beautiful pieces are the curlier ones. It is also used for the white keys of the piano. It is seldom used in guitars, for, as in the case of rosewood, it does not produce the great classic sound.

Cypress

Cypress is light yellow in color, has a straight grain, growth rings, a shiny texture, and a fragrant smell. Its weight is approximately 500 kg/m. This wood, slow in growth, has a height of 30 to 35 meters, and a diameter of 80 to 190 centimeters. Since it is a tree with many branches and not a very long trunk, it is difficult to extract clean, straight wood to use in our guitars. The beautiful cypress is traditionally used for the flamenco guitar, which is different from the classical guitar in color, weight, and the way it is played. The flamenco guitar is plucked with more speed, strummed, played staccato, and requires the use of the thumb. In short, it needs action closer to the fingerboard, with a shorter distance in the height between the strings and the frets. Therein lies one of the difficulties of a great flamenco guitar: that it must be mild in sound, easy to play, its sound must come out as clearly as possible, and its strings should not screech.

Since the beginning of the century, cypress has been highly prized by Madrid guitar makers who have been more interested in the flamenco guitar than anyone else in the world. It can almost be said that this is one of the most romantic concerns of the trade.

Cupressus spp.
Family: Cupressaceae
EAST AFRICAN CYPRESS (S)

Aranjuez, in the Madrid Autonomous Region, is an industrial town with a lot of agricultural wealth, since the Tajo River passes through it. In the 16th century it served as the royal residence and a private game reserve. Among its monuments, we can clearly distinguish the Royal Palace and its fascinating gardens which, from the time of the Catholic Monarchs to the reign of Carlos IV, became one of the biggest concerns of the royalty. They were interested in seeing these gardens become fertile grounds, where a great variety of species could develop and grow; such as this magnificent soaring cypress with a strong trunk and open branches. In order to take care of and protect the garden and the palace, a state administrative heritage office was created. Among its numerous buildings was a sawmill that sold woods from trees that had fallen down from natural causes. Occasionally, one of these marvellous century-old cypresses would collapse. And since this wood is not used by anyone in the wood industry (cabinetmakers, carpenters,) only guitar makers would then acquire it.

Between 1939 and 1959, I paid several visits to Aranjuez. On the last occasion, I went to buy wood with Marcelo Barbero, taking advantage of an invitation by a flamenco variety show company, which was to perform in the bullfighting ring, to accompany them in their coach.

We went to the sawmill where we chose and bought our cypress. We arranged for its transportation to another sawmill in Madrid where we had it made into chunks and pieces to be, once dry, cut into the right thickness for the sides and backs of our flamenco guitars. Incidentally, this was the very last time my dear friend and brother Marcelo visited Aranjuez, for he died on 6 March 1956. That last visit must have taken place in the autumn of 1955. I still have several pieces from that cypress, which I left in Madrid before moving to Los Angeles. Out of this carefully conserved material it is still possible to construct at least a dozen marvellous flamenco guitars.

Beautiful Rosewood (Brazil)

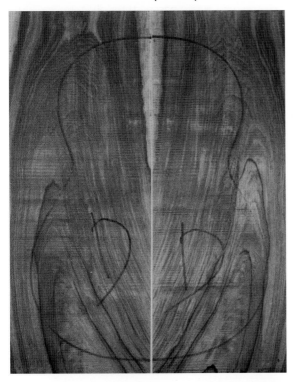

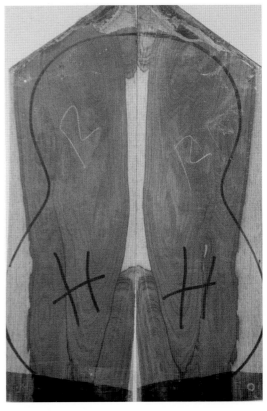

Guitar backs

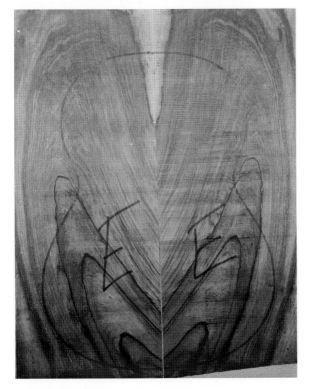

2.2. Our Woods: From Yesterday to the Present Day

The wars—the Spanish Civil War and then World War II—dealt a devastating blow in general, and nearly everything had to be started anew.

For a long time, Germany was the main supplier of materials for the musical instrument construction industry—from all kinds of wood to every accessory for our guitars.

At the beginning of the 1950s, a few bright guys were already bringing in their cars certain articles that were beginning to be available in Europe. Among the articles that started reaching us from Germany were quality soundboards, gears, frets, etc.

I well remember Dotras Córdoba, a trader who would show us various products and soundboards from Germany that became the hope at our workshops on Ministriles Street. Not to mention my friend Mr. Donntag, a chemist in the textile industry and a great guitar aficionado, who was also bringing us soundboards and colored veneer woods for our mosaic. I still have some of those veneers from the '50s and, I must say, they are the best wood dyes I have ever seen.

However, today the business initiative that has prevailed and had honored our industry is the Barber Company. Its beginning dates back to the time when my friend Rafael Barber, a German language student in 1958, was working in Germany over the summer. Prior to his trip to Germany, he passed through Madrid and visited his aunt, the famous Laura Requena, a bookseller and the owner of "La Casa de la Troya" at 83 San Bernardo Street. Any student in Madrid in those years remembers this bookshop, which still exists today. This lady's brother—who earned a living by creating inexpensive guitars, and for whom we repaired some instruments at Ministriles street— was aware of our precarious situation in wood purchase, and called on Rafael Barber to provide us with wood to construct our instruments.

On returning from Germany at the end of the summer, Rafael Barber brought some top-quality German pinewood, which many liked and of which he took maximum advantage. As the industry was short of good materials, Barber, a good native of Valencia—a land of trading—started bringing in wood in his humble Fiat 1100. Seeing the profits that he could make and the conditions of the Valencia industry, Barber and his brothers became wholesalers and began buying large soundboards of different qualities. Some were sold to the industry; the most suitable ones ended up with guitar makers.

They moved to one of their parents' warehouses and started importing the woods that we use today to create our guitars: ebony trunks, Honduran Cedar, Indian and Brazilian Rosewoods, trumpet woods, and various accessories. It then became necessary for them to set up their own sawmill on Oriente Street, Valencia. That was in 1966, and the business was booming; all of which allowed the guitar industry in Spain to enhance the quality of its instruments, thanks to the good woods available at the Barbers' warehouses.

In June 1969, Rafael Barber died, and the family asked Luis Barber, who was reading philosophy at the University of Valencia at the time, to take charge of the running of the business. Today, Luis Barber, with his wood culture and talent; his wife, Charo de Barber, with her keen intelligence and practical sense; and their friend Vaseli and the rest of his collaborators, run this wood store for our guitars—the only one in the industry and the first in the world.

With Vaseli, Luis Barber trots the globe, cutting and obtaining wood. His wife, Charo de Barber, self-taught, has created veneers with Sapeli, Brazilian Rosewood, and other woods that are today indispensable to the construction of guitars—given that they guarantee the durability of the instruments; durability which can certainly not be provided by solid wood, which easily breaks and warps. Thanks to these veneers, our guitars have the beauty of the wood with its grain and natural color, giving them a bright and colorful appearance.

As a veteran luthier guitar maker of the past and present, I am really proud to be able to have this rich range of wood at my disposal, from which I can choose top quality pieces for my guitars. I admire the Barber family for their initiative and courage; and for the present efforts of Charo and Luis in bringing such varied treasure that provides us with so many possibilities to choose from.

2.3. Beyond the Cut: Will There Be Enough Wood?

The million-dollar question is whether there will be enough wood for future generations to appreciate and enjoy, considering their beauty and value to those who work and create with them. Or whether, on the contrary, there will be a hunger for or a shortage of wood—at least the woods that I know—as we enjoy them today.

What is certain is that the woods that I have come to know—and of which I have samples—could only be known about through books and their illustrations, or maybe through some vestiges of the past—for instance, a natural piece that might have been preserved.

The good fortune of my generation lies partly in having had wood in its natural form, in trunks, and in cutting and working with it. Happily, in countries with a higher level of economic development, the yearning and tendency for reforestation is today a very civilized practice. In the future, we shall be able to rely on wood that grows in Europe, North America, and Canada. In this dear country of mine, Spain, there are unfortunately more forest fires than

BEYOND
THE CUT

reforestation. There exist vast stretches of land which are no longer used for sowing, but could be reforested. In South America, the richest area in exotic woods—I call them "precious" woods, because of their beautiful grain and colors—the devastation is somewhat beyond repair, depriving the world of this generosity of Nature.

In the future, the best policy will be to take good care of our woods; a must for the survival of the planet. Science will have to make great efforts in the biological conservation of species, and in the selection and better growth of our woods in the different parts of the planet. The costs can be offset by the great value of solid wood. At present, even trees of the least valued species are exploited to the fullest, including their tiniest branches— a result of crushed-wood and chipboard production. But none of this better utilization of wood (for instance the chipboard) can be of use in our musical instruments— especially our guitar. The only thing that they can be used for—and we are the most economical in this—is the veneered backs and sides. These backs and sides are made up of three 7/10 veneers of Indian Rosewood. It is utopian to think of the use of solid wood for economically priced guitars.

The use of solid wood for guitars requires perfect drying to ensure the highest guarantee of the instrument, instrument's quality of soundboard, backs, sides, neck, and fingerboard. We must reduce its humidity to at least 4%, and it requires a certain amount of airing time for its subsequent oxidation.

In my experience, the woods we use today are more stable than ever. In the past, the necks and the fingerboards became warped, and the backs and the soundboards ended up splitting. At the workshop where I worked, there even was a handyman who dedicated his time exclusively to repairs. Guitars of today do not undergo anywhere near the 10% deterioration rate of those days.

I am frankly moved when I contemplate this element of nature that gives life to the planet. The tree: its beauty, its oxygen, the shade that it gives us, and its marvellous product which is the wood, in its multiplicity of uses, qualities, and its support in making man's passage through life more pleasant.

We, my family and I, are proud to be tree planters who take good care of them and have the satisfaction of working with its product, its wood. In my countless trips by road throughout Europe and North America, I have had the pleasure of seeing an instrument played in the shade of a tree, while I take shelter under large fir trees, cedars, sequoias, acers, and many more species.

In Europe, Canada, and North America, travelling on the highways is a pleasure that satisfies the spirit and renews the love for Nature. The scenic sights provided by their forests are absolutely marvellous. All along the way, you can appreciate their various stages: youth, maturity, the desolation of the felled forests, and the hope implied in the new shoots planted as "baby trees."

2.4. The Art of, and the Need for Varnishing the Guitar

Humidity and Wood

As we all know, wood undergoes a variety of alterations from the time the tree is felled until it can be used in its many applications. For the wood to be usable, its humidity must be reduced to the barest minimum.

Humid wood warps, shrinks, and undergoes changes that may put into danger anything constructed with it. Its weight drops when it dries out. For example, a fresh piece of wood weighing 30 kg will, after one week of a mechanical drying process, weigh 5 kg or less.

The thing is that wood cells are minute cavities—imagine a beehive—with water inside of them. When the tree is experiencing full growth, water is found within the cells as well as in the walls.

When a tree is cut down, the wood is like a sponge full of water, which is why, in order for the wood to be used, it becomes necessary to apply pressure somehow, so as to force the water to drain out.

As a point of interest, I can tell you that the wood we use today for the soundboards of our guitars, which get the best results in harmonic features, is the so-called Western Red Cedar (*Thuja plicata*). When being cut into pieces for the soundboards of our guitars, it is necessary to saw them when humid rather than dry. The explanation is that the water inside this wood, which it is not resinous, serves as a lubricant and makes it easier to cut.

Thuja plicata, when used in our guitars, poses a great danger for the one who works without adequate protection, owing to the inhalation of sawdust. Sanding this cedar, once dry, produces extremely fine sawdust which, when mixed with the air, can seriously harm the bronchi and the lungs. Hence the indispensable use of masks. Fortunately, all of us who work with this wood are cognizant of this problem and take the necessary precautions. All the same, some veterans are today ill after having worked in the past with this wood. Currently, there are mechanical ovens with precise computerized controls that dry the wood to maximum effect, making it sweat to an optimum point. The last contribution to the "perfect sweating" process consists of a long period of exposure in the open air. This way, the wood is guaranteed for the sale of these instruments in any part of the planet.

Manuel Rodriguez I,
using French polish, 1941.

In constructing guitars, the traditional luthier never makes use of mechanical methods. We buy the wood in its natural state—tree trunks—and after some years, we convert them into boards by cutting them into quarter—cuts in order to maintain the quality of their grain and smoothness. Subsequently, they are cut into various pieces for the different guitar parts: soundboards, backs, sides, necks, and inside elements.

Diametrically opposed to the luthier is the manufacturer, who has to dry the woods for his instruments by mechanical means. The great number of guitars that he has to produce warrants this method. The luthier only dries his wood by natural means, in the open air and in the specified time period. And it is precisely these years of drying and storage of his woods that serve as the great incentive for the luthier. He must know how to preserve them with great zeal and esteem, so that the instruments he constructs with these woods, mainly top-quality ones—and in many cases unrepeatable ones—never suffer from any of the adverse effects of either humidity or a hot, wet draught that may make nonsense of the glues and cause the wood to warp.

However, the protection of wood in general, and that of musical instruments in particular, is achieved through varnishing. By polishing the wood, you protect it, embellish it, preserve its color; you enhance its natural appearance and the caprice in its design of its grain, and, in doing so, you highlight its beauty. Smoothing down and polishing the wood is also a way of protecting it from the reversals and rigors of nature: humidity and the ultraviolet rays of the sun. Besides, by polishing wood, you enhance its appearance and "gloss over" its growth defects. Varnishing musical instruments is, therefore, a science and an art, requiring good taste plus experience in balance and color.

The purpose and reason for varnishing, as I have explained, really has to do with appearance. However, it is also for the durability and maintenance of the instruments. The varnish protects the wood by introducing light materials into its pores, impeding the entry of humidity. It beautifies its appearance and, what is more, improves the sound qualities of the instrument. Throughout history, all prestigious luthiers have concluded, in no uncertain terms, that every musical instrument constructed from wood (violins, lutes, guitars, etc.) needs to be varnished. Nevertheless, initially, a stringed instrument made from unvarnished wood sounds louder and has a better quality sound in its virgin state. Shortly after being played, its qualities change—especially so in its tone and volume, which become poorer and weaker.

In its application, too much varnish will badly affect the vibrations; too little will not provide any protection. The balance in the use of varnish and its polishing—done exquisitely and manually—converts the appearance of the instrument into a work of art. The only instruments that are not comparable with our guitar are the bowed stringed instruments. Like the violin luthier, the guitar maker's ambition is to create a precious musical instrument with high-quality sound. Varnish provides the instrument's precious appearance and ensures its optimum preservation.

But the varnishing of the violin has centuries of history and is shrouded in secrecy, albeit with extraordinary results. This explains the longevity of these instruments, which have lasted up to our day. In the guitar, by contrast, the protection of the instrument by means of varnish has been, in many an instance, archaic. There has always been reliance on varnishes that are easy to use, such as shellac or alcohol. But let me say it once again: the *raison d'être* of varnishing is to protect the instrument from the climatic temperatures. Humidity may be defined as the amount of water particles in the atmosphere and their absorption by the wood. Humidity in varnish will cause cloudiness and shady patches. It will cause the grain to swell and will slow down the drying time of the varnish. Nevertheless, extreme dryness will cause the varnish to harden and possibly crack. The idea is that every pore of the different woods used in constructing our instrumenst should be well covered and closed up. Thus, the covering of the pores is of vital importance. The varnishers of the past, such as Santos, Esteso, and my father (who used shellac), and some varnishers today, would cover the wood pores with pumice stone powder.

The Stradivarius house-workshop in Cremona. Note the attic where instruments are dried and varnished.

Pumice stone powder is also, and has always been, used in violin lutherie. We grind the pumice stone until we obtain a very fine powder. The choice of the pumice stone has justification; its light weight. Once soaked in alcohol and with the aid of a *muñequilla*—a piece of cotton wool or cotton cloth of about five centimeters in diameter—it is forced into the pores. It is also employed in hand varnishing—a laborious operation—to get a coating thick enough to cover up the pores and form a quality and glossy film that preserves the wood in its optimum state.

In some cases, the absorption of the pumice stone is not one hundred per cent; so after time and the drying process, the wood would look dirty, as if dyed with a certain greyish color on the inside. This does not happen in the violin family and bowed stringed instruments, as they are colored and the wood, maple acer, is not as porous as our rosewood and cedar.

In varnishing pinewoods, it has always been considered that the absorption of humidity is too difficult, in that the varnish's own humidity raises the grain in the wood. Most luthiers usually impregnate the wood with either linseed oil or olive oil. The old masters would make a mixture of olive oil and vinegar as a means of protecting the wood.

After the pores have been covered with a light and colorless material, those varnishes that have been applied only superficially have absolutely no

Habra un silencio verde todo hecho de guitarras destrenzadas.

La guirarra es un pozo con viento en vex de agua.

G. DIEGO

subsequent effects on the tone, quality, and volume of the sound. That is, as long as the varnish is not very thick and several coatings have been applied. It has been proved that, especially in soundboards made of pine, impregnating with oil makes it penetrate into the wood cells and substitutes the water inside them with oil, which, upon drying and oxidizing, lightens the weight of the soundboard and improves its sound quality.

In the work of J. Michelman, *Violin Varnish* (1946), he affirms that impregnating the whole instrument with linseed oil will produce the following result:

Original weight of violin	291.96 g.
Oil used in impregnating	7.7 g.
Violin impregnated with oil	299. 2 g.
Weight of violin imbued with oil when dry	———— 286.6 g.

In the above case, the oil was applied with a violin brush. Then it was left in the sun for four days, (two days with the case covered and two days uncovered) in a horizontal position, and in a case with a glass top. At the very initial stages of the experiment, a certain mistiness was observed in the glass case, which implied that the oil was entering into the pores of the wood and the water inside the cells was evaporating and being replaced by the oil, which upon drying became oxidized.

The difference between the violin luthier and the guitar luthier is due to the fact that in bowed stringed instruments the varnish plays an important and vital role in their sound and preservation; an absolute science in the preparation, application, drying, and polishing processes.

For years, the determination of the luthier of bowed stringed instruments has been to build his violins, cellos, etc. with varnish, so as to create a solid base that would protect his instruments and give them an advantage. This, in part, is the reason why today there exist magnificent violins, violas, and cellos that are hundreds of years old, with unique sounds and beautiful appearances, and in perfect states of preservation that still conserve the color and shine of their extraordinary varnishes. The difference is significant. The fact is, the violinist does not even rub the body of these bowed stringed instruments, whereas the guitarist literally embraces every part of the instrument.

The varnish used in a stringed instrument is, therefore, an integral part of it. Naturally, the instrument is distinguished by the choice of woods, by the painstaking construction of its quality decoration, and the precision of the work.

In the bowed stringed instrument family, what counts is the line, the distinction of the curves, and how delicate the headstock is. Varnish never enhances an instrument that is badly created with poor-quality wood and defective construction.

Cuando digo madera, digo guitarra
porque el árbol transido de esplendores
y abrumado de cigarras,
se hizo caja sonora hacia los vientos
viajeros del alba.
        ARCIPRESTE DE HITA

Jose Ramirez Workshop, 1925
My father, seated, varnishing a guitar, as Antonio Gómez works at the bench.

2.5. Varnishes: Yesterday and Today

Varnish is made up of organic matter and solvent. As they mix together, they form a viscous liquid that becomes the varnish. Once the varnish evaporates, a thin film is formed on the wood. When the film dries up and hardens, it protects and embellishes the wood.

Nowadays, there are countless varieties of varnish. Its components are resins derived from various products: acrylic, alkyd, acetate cellulose, nitro-cellulose, oils of all kinds, puelonycil, polyester, polyurethane, film, shellac, urea, and vinyl. There are others that evaporate easily and form a film: lac, shellac, water-acrylic varnishes, poliacrylic, and polyurethane.

Shellac is probably the oldest of the lot. Shellac is a compound of resins—insects and their excrement accumulated on various tree branches (acacia, fig tree, etc.) in the southeastern regions of Asia. Insects feed on the tree sap and deposit it on the leaf. When it forms a layer of resin and carcasses, ten millimeters thick, the branches covered with this matter are collected in resin rods. The raw resin rods contain a vivid red matter: ink that is extracted through washing. When dry, the residue becomes granular. These granules are melted and solidified into drops, which break up and form the flakes that we know. These flakes, which are very red and orangish in color, are what we call shellac. Currently, there are various types on the market: natural, brownish-red, orange, ruby, and a colorless one that has been artificially bleached.

Shellac is 85–95% soluble in alcohol, 13–15% in ether, 10–20% in benzol, and 2–6% in benzene. It hardly dissolves in turpentine and it is impossible to be diluted with water

In a nutshell, shellac is not a resin in a pure state like others that will be mentioned below. The 16th-century luthiers had absolutely no knowledge of chemistry, but they did possess the technique for creating varnish for their instruments—which we admire today and will still admire for a long time to come.

All the masters of the Cremona epoch in Italy had the same formula for their instruments' varnish. Their results were not the outcome of any fantasy or magical science, but rather that of their keen sense of their times and the materials that were available in their environment. Their sight, touch, and even their noses helped discover resources that their understanding and skill dictated to them could be used for the creation of their instruments.

The materials used in those days were none other than natural pine resin, linseed oil, olive oil, and others. The varnishes of the Italian luthier-masters of the 16th and 17th centuries, when the natives of Cremona, Stradivari, Amati, and Guarneri produced their masterpieces, were materials that were at that time indigenous to the areas where they carried out their trade.

As their forefathers had done, these masters made their own colors, creating their varnishes with oils, acrylics, resin, ashes, roots, etc. These materials, which were the only ones available, are still in normal use even today.

Linseed oil was, and still is, one of the main components used by luthiers (this is also true for the great painters), plus certain mineral salts such as potassium carbonate, which is made by brewing animal and plant oils, ashes, and roots.

Another essential ingredient was pine resin. This resin, good quality and transparent, was boiled to make it purer. (I imagine the purity of the water of the springs in the 15th and 16th centuries would be beyond question.) Today, the water has to be distilled, then salts and potassium carbonate added to the boiling. To hasten its precipitation, aluminum chloride and calcium chloride are added to the boiling liquid, in equal proportion. The resin melts and a viscous liquid is produced. This liquid becomes a paste, which, once dry, will be made into aresin powder free from impurities and acids. That is the main material of this varnish, which is proportionally made up of this resin, linseed oil and turpentine. This is the varnish to use. (You know, I am telling it here just as I was told). This is the formula with which the great 15th-century luthiers were supposed to have varnished their instruments. I have been using it, and I am satisfied with it. Well, I will have more to say about that later.

Varnishes of Today, Consequence of the Past

Brush Varnishing

Like any other tool, the brush is an extension of its user. The best way to use the brush is to hold one side with the thumb and the other with the other four fingers, just like an extension of the hand. It is dipped into the varnish and applied very gently, without pressing hard, and with the brush always moving in both directions.

Here is a selection of varnishes that may be used for our guitars:

1. **Shellac:** dries in 30 minutes, very fragile, not very durable, excellent adhesion, very easy to apply.

2. **Lac:** dries in 20 minutes, very fragile.

3. **Nitrocellulose:** more durable, excellent adhesion, very easy to apply.

4. **Oil varnish:** dries in 6 hours, more resistant, quite durable, very good adhesion, very fragile.

5. **Polyurethane varnish:** dries in 6 hours, very flexible, very good durability, very good adhesion, easy to apply.

French Polishes

As explained before, the *muñequilla* is a piece of cotton cloth dipped in varnish and then covered with another cloth of the same material.

The usual way to go about French polishing is as follows: the muñequilla is dipped in the varnish, and for the first coating, is passed all over the surface in up-and-down movements so as to spread out the varnish. This also serves as a first adhesive. Then every time you dip it in the varnish, you must put a few drops of oil on it to serve as a lubricant. Caution: not too many drops, because at the end of the process, the muñequilla and the oil (which may either be olive oil, linseed oil, mineral oil, or others) have to be washed out. The polishing is done with a circular action. Always remember that, after every 3 or 4 coatings, the muñequilla, together with the oil or lubricant, is dipped in alcohol, the better to spread out the varnish and the oil.

Varnishes suitable for French polishing:

1. **Shellac:** dries in 10 minutes, poor durability, excellent adhesion, easy to apply.

2. **Oil polyurethane:** dries in 2 hours, flexible, poor durability, excellent adhesion, easy to apply.

3. **Nitrocellulose lac:** This French polish still exists on the market today. Its quality is neither superior nor inferior to that of the other French polishes, although it is possibly less flexible. It dries in 20 minutes and is easy to use.

Spray Varnishing

This is the most common system of varnishing used today. The biggest difference between spray varnishing and brush and French polishing is that, with the spray, the varnish is uniformly spread out on the area to be varnished.

To use this method, an air compressor is needed, which will at least require industrial equipment. This is the only reason why many luthier varnishers who work on their instruments would rather use the brush or the French polish. Well, I have to confess that in all my long experience, in the case of the guitar, spray varnishing is much more durable. It provides better protection for the wood and makes the precious wood we use for our guitars appear to have more glow.

Varnishes suitable for spraying guitars:

1. **Shellac** (special for spray): dries in 10 minutes, very fragile, normal durability, excellent adhesion, easy to use.

2. **Nitrocellulose lac:** brittle, quite durable, excellent adhesion, easy to use.

3. **Urethane:** dries in 10 minutes on contact; the next coating must be done 12 hours later. It is very flexible, has excellent adhesion, and is very suitable for spraying.

The Golden Lustre

Instruments: The little wooden musical instrument; the high and stately violin.

There is no doubt that the violin is a magnificent instrument with unequalled qualities. This notwithstanding, the difficulty for a single violin to be heard by even those in the distant seats of a huge, modern auditorium is the lament of the modern-day orchestra. If this occurs with the violin, despite its far-reaching sound, it goes without saying that the guitar has no part to play in the world of the full orchestra. But my interest in this article, in connection with the guitar, is closely related to the learned opinions of eminent world-acclaimed luthiers.

The "Golden Lustre": the biggest mystery of varnish. In the opinion of Desmond Hill, the knowledgeable and experienced connoisseur, varnish is important because it impacts the absorption of sound. If the varnish is very hard, the sound is fragile and weak. If the varnish is too soft, the sound comes out very heavy with hardly any brilliance—in other words, the varnishing causes the sound to come out "mellow" (typical of shellac). This mellow sound is very pleasant and easy to listen to, and ideal for indoor gatherings and ballroom concerts, but it is highly unsuitable for a commercial auditorium. That is why, in my opinion, a flexible and modern varnish, intelligently applied, helps to produce a brilliant sound, while at the same time providing a good protection for the instrument. Just as with violins constructed by immortal authors, the duration and the preservation of the instrument is the dream to which every luthier aspires.

Chapter 3

Construction Technique

Allí sale gritando la guitarra morisca,
En voces aguda y áspera en notas;
El ventrudo laúd que acompaña a la triste;
La guitarra hispana con éstos se junta

GANIVET

3.1. Other Stringed Musical Instruments in Spain

Other names for what is commonly known as the "lute" are the "tanbu" and the "oud."

The master of this instrument, Ziryad, who introduced an additional string made of animal gut, took this lute to Al-Andalus. "The strings are made of silk that has not been spun with hot water, which makes them feminine and soft. The third and the fourth strings are made of lion's guts, softer and more sonorous than those from any other animal," he states in his treatises. He would color these strings to symbolize the human body's humors: the first was yellow and represented the bile; the second was red, representing blood; the third was white, representing phlegm; the fourth was black, representing black bile.

He also used an ostrich quill as a plectrum, as he was always in search of a more sonorous and softer sound.

The most ancient documented dipiction of the oud is found on an ivory vase made by an artist from Córdoba in 968 BC. It is in the Louvre.

In Andalusia, the authentic luthiers (could there be a more fitting name for lute makers?) created and developed the use of the rosette on the sound-board, or the soundhole as it is now called.

The North African countries to the west of Egypt preferred the Greek word "guitarra," which was adapted into Arabic before the year 1000 (together with many other musical terms developed by the Greeks). In the Arab world, the oud was used as accompaniment to percussive dance music.

The Lute up to This Day

The Archpriest of Hita makes mention of the in his book, *Libro de Buen Amor*, and although it is a mere reference, it is the precursor instrument of the lute we have today.

The oud of Andalusia, developed sometime after the 5th, is the fruit that feeds the musical interpretation of the folklore, dances, and songs of the different regions of Spain.

It can be said that the companion of the oud throughout the centuries was the banduria, which was also cited by the Archpriest of Talavera and recalled by Fernan Ruiz of Seville in 1500.

In an inventory taken in 1602 of Felipe II's properties and treasures, mention is made of a 4-stringed banduria, with a juniper top and natural tortoiseshell body. P. Trichet (1640) says in his treatise that originally, the "mandore" had four strings, then five or six. On occasion, it had double strings

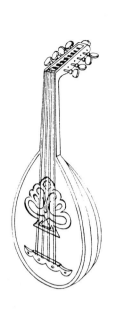
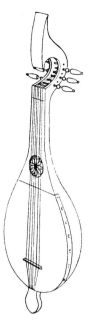
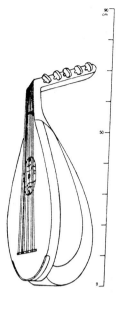

A. Arabic lute from the Middle Ages. Vienna Museum.
B. Egyptian lute from the Middle Ages. Vienna Museum.
C. Russian kopza (kobsa). Berlin Museum.

Bandura Ukranian

Banduria Española de
A. Viudes (1890).

just as the banduria or lute of today. Likewise, Father Bermudo makes reference to it in his *Declaration of Musical Instruments* of 1556. The fact is that, in the 16th century, the banduria was one of the leading instruments of the renaissance orchestra; which makes us believe that before and after the 16th century, this instrument was played in conjunction with other instruments, as it is nowadays.

If we were to fold the map of Europe into two, on one end would be Russia; and, strangely enough, in Ukraine, Mongolia, and Tartar, one can find the "bandura." Descended from the Ukrainian "korza," the bandura appeared in that country at the beginning of the 12th century, on the Tartar border of Crimea. It was also very popular in Poland. Originally, it had 8 and 13 strings, and later on, 18 and 20 strings. Given the great variety of 16th- and 17th-century lutes, one could also mention the "angelica," with 16 strings, and others such as the alto lute with 11 strings, and the tenor lute and the bass lute, with different string thicknesses and scales.

The Russian-Ukrainian korza-bandura, like the lute and other instruments of the Middle Ages, were as capricious of form as of construction, and in most cases, were constructed by the musician himself for his own use. (That is why one can find different stringing methods and strings of very different scale and thickness.) With the lute, ordinary men celebrated their bonanzas, festivals, ceremonies, and family gatherings. They used it in their folklore, dances, choirs, and religious observations.

Lute and present day banduria.

Today these plucking-and-plectrum instruments, developed over the centuries, are greatly admired for their richness of sound and musical variety, and for the wonders they evoke when an accompaniment to singing and dancing—a legacy of our folklore.

The korza, or Ukrainian banduria (or bandura), similar to our "calvete," is more similar to the typical Portuguese guitar than to our more traditional pear-shaped banduria. The strings are tied to the headstock, more or less as in the violin and with a similar scroll. The bridge is a strip of wood with which one adjusts the string scale. The strings are tied to a tailpiece on the end block of the instrument, known in musical language as "end block," which is the part where the sides join together.

By way of an anecdote, Mr. L. Haydamaka says that, "among the many out-standing instrumentalists of this Ukrainian banduria, Professor H. Khotkevich outshone the others as a talented composer and writer for this instrument. Also he excelled as a performer of great purity in folk music, and was as well a singer and a banduria soloist." From 1925 to 1936, Professor Khotkevich gave banduria classes at the conservatory in the city of Kharkov to many a disciple who would, in turn, become a distinguished player of this instrument. "In 1936 he was arrested, and that was last we heard of him," concludes Haydamaka.

Plucking and Plectrum Instruments: Their Orchestras, Serenade Troupes, Trios, Quartets, and Soloists.

In my experience as a luthier who constructs guitars, bandurias, and lutes, I can say that half-way through my professional life (1943–1959) in Madrid, as well as in other provinces, especially in Zaragoza and other Aragón cities, the serenade troupes flourished as accompanists to the enchanting and virile jota singers and dancers.

In Andalusia, they provided music for their "zambras" (Gypsy festivities characterized by lots of dancing), in those very flamenco caves of Granada, which no longer exist. Also in the sevillanas dancing, they provided guitar, banduria, and lute accompaniment.

3.2. Guitar-Making: Tools, Frets, and Their Distribution

To make bandurias and lutes, we used the most commonplace tools of the wood trade. I shall enumerate them in order of importance: a plane, its blade, and blade holder (for sharpening), and a jack plane. You can do almost everything with this plane: gluing the bracings, the neck, the fingerboard and all that is required for construction, such as the carving of the fingerboard, and gluing and the levelling of the bridge. This plane is made of oak, usually bought second-hand, since the wood has to be very dry to get the best out of it. The medium-sized jack plane is also made of old oak. With this medium-sized jack plane, an indispensable tool, we make the joints—the very precise and precious joints. First, the soundboard joint is constructed, and this has to be flawless and of higher resistance than the wood itself. It is followed by the back, which is also precision work, and then the sides which have to be cut in a straight line, depending on the width. This medium-sized jack plane is also used for rough-planing the wood of the necks. It is also very useful in determining their width and thickness. As I mentioned before, we use the plane for gluing. The jack plane is indispensable in the rough-planing of the fingerboard, in determining its thickness, and, as I have said, in making the fingerboard straight.

The fine plane is very useful in the fundamental operation of cutting the tops to the proper thickness—one of the most delicate operations carried out by the luthier. Tops made of pine and Canadian cedar are most common these days and there is a wide range of types: some are wide-grained, very stiff, and heavy; some have the same grain-width in the top, and these are very flexible and light. The same is true for those of thin, close grain. The ideal one, the kind that makes a good top stand out, has a very fine grain, is very straight, is stiff , and light in weight. This kind is not very common, and is therefore used in the more expensive instruments. In my opinion, a wide-grain top with the same width throughout the soundboard will produce a top-quality and respectable sound. It will also be light in weight and quite stiff. As you will understand, the luthier has a challenge before him: to obtain the suitable width for the kind of sound required by the instrument he is constructing.

As I said, to obtain the right thickness for the soundboard, the oakwood fine-plane is used. To plane the top to the proper thickness, we rely on the carving table. This table consists of a 5-centimeter thick piece of hard vermil-ion wood, 50 cm in width by about 80 cm in length, give and take—that is the size of mine. We bought this table, which came originally from Guinea, in the mid-1940s, and it is still very useful today.

These are the measurements of my table. The tables of Santos Hernández and Marcelo Barbero that I saw were lighter, narrower, and not as thick. Maestro Santos Hernández had two tables for carving wood to the required thickness: the short and wide one was used for tops and backs, and the long and narrow one for the sides.

With this table and the plane, we would intuitively obtain the required thickness, since the present-day gauges did not exist in our day. As Torres would say, "The secret of my guitars lies in the sensitiveness of my fingers." Special note should be taken of the great diversity and difference in the wood used in making the soundboards of our instruments. The variety in wood is so vast that scientists proclaim its changes and achievement as noteworthy,

The Luthier's Tools

Chisels

Planes

Files

Bramils

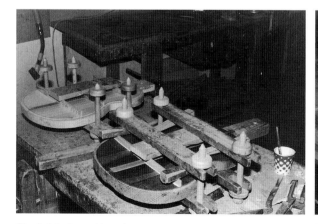

The luthier's workbench

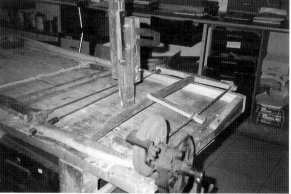

Hand saw

but without giving it the expected importance. Such are the imponderable factors that are overlooked by our scholarly friends.

Next on the tools list are the saws. As the story goes, both Saint Joseph and Christ used them in their day. The saw is a steel blade with teeth. We had two: one had a wide blade (3 cm and the other a narrow blade, 5 mm). To saw thick wood, the wide blade is of little or no use, and the narrow blade is used for rounding. These two saws have long handles: 4 cm wide by 60 cm long. Another handle of the same width (4 cm) passes through both saws at the extreme ends, joining them in the middle. The saw is held on one end, a rope is tied on the opposite end, and there is a kind of a stick in the middle that can be turned to loosen or tighten the saws.

Throughout the centuries, all kinds of wooden objects have been constructed with these types of saws, which have even been powered by electricity and steam, both of which led to the creation of machines. The young people of today are not familiar with them; they know them only through books. These books illustrate the felling and cutting of huge tree trunks by oversized saws with enormous teeth, pulled by a strong-bodied woodcutter on one side and another on the opposite side.

The most significant tools for the luthier guitar maker are the bramils. There are two types: square and round. The square bramil is the one that traces and cuts. It marks out the box for the purfling, the groove for the gears, the bridges, and multiple tracings. It cuts all that has a veneer: 2.5-mm top-sound-hole veneer, 7-mm purfling veneer, the strips of wood inside the soundboard, and everything that is not more than 2 mm thick. By contrast, with the round bramil we can only do one thing: its sole function is to trace and chisel out the grooves for the soundhole veneer and mosaic. The 2-mm chisel is used for chiselling out grooves. After tracing, chiselling out the grooves, inlaying, veneering, and mosaicking, this plane goes into action to get a properly sized soundhole. The function of the soundhole bramil ends here.

The chisels are naturally of various sizes, especially in width. The 3-cm one especially is used for rough-hewing the neck-body joint. The others: 2 cm, 1.5 cm, 1 cm, and the thin ones up to 2 mm (the last mentioned is for our exclusive use:, as the thinnest that is manufactured measures 4 mm; we reduce these to 2 cm ourselves).

The fine scraping blades are used in various operations in guitar construction. They are among the most indispensable tools for the guitar maker. They are usually bought from the saw grinder. For me, they are ideal. Large-sized handsaws (4 or 5 meters), are usually 5–7cm wide. The teeth are cut off, and what is left is a 12 x 5-cm blade. We curve them slightly, sharpen them, and cut them short at both ends, leaving a bit of a bevelled edge. These blades come in very handy. They are used during the carving and thicknessing of backs, sides and tops, and also for fine-planing the guitar after all the parts have been glued together, and before the sanding of the instrument to get it ready for varnishing.

As you can expect, the neck is the most complex part of the guitar. In the Spanish school, every part of the classical guitar is built in conjunction with the neck and in line with it, which means using quite a number of delicate tools to develop such an important part.

As already stated, in creating the neck, your first ally is the jack plane, which rough-hews it to the proper width and thickness. Then the fine plane is used to make the neck-body and the headstock joints. Next come the 20-cm screws. Remember, back when I started out—and I know this because I personally lived it and witnessed it, as did such luthiers as Santos Hernández, Marcelo Barbero, Ramírez, etc.—these iron screws were not used. What we used were strings and wedges. On the neck, the headstock is held by means of string and wedges, as is the headstock-body joint. While we are still on the subject of the string and wedges, it is necessary to say that these two elements are most indispensable when it comes to constructing guitars by hand. The use of string is a must even today in industrial construction—much more so in handcrafted guitars—during the gluing of the purfling on the edges, tops, and the backs of the guitars, bandurias, and lutes.

Many are those who have racked their brains in search of the best system for gluing these purflings. Until the end of the 1990s, nothing was found, neither a machine nor a system, that could replace the string in this fundamental operation. The strings and wedges are indispensable for joining the cover and the back. Together with sticks specifically made for this operation, they are the only means for creating our guitar. The bridge and the fingerboard are also glued to the neck with the aid of the string and the wedge.

Other indispensable tools are the joining and pressing sticks. These sticks, generally made of good and hard wood, measure 60 x 5 x 2.5 cm. Mine are made of beechwood. At both ends, a cut, 1.5 cm deep and 7 cm long, is made in the center. This cut is necessary as it helps the string hold the joints tight and also serves as an entry for the press screws. These sticks are very necessary when it comes to joining the backs and the tops by hand. With string and a wedge (60 x 4 x 4), the sticks are placed parallel to one another. A piece of paper is put at the point where the joint brushes against the stick, to prevent the stick from touching the back. After that, the two veneers are glued together and tied with the string. Starting from the extreme ends, the stick is tied by interweaving the string around it at least six times. Then the wedge is placed so that it presses hard against the instrument, and the two veneers are joined together.

The pressing sticks are used with the wooden screws for fixing the sides, the top, and the neck; plus, with two of these screws and two sticks, we form a press, which we use for gluing the bracings of the soundboard, as well as the three or four sticks on the back.

Another useful utensil for the craftsman is the joining table. This 1 x 15 cm table has another strip of wood, 1 x 5 x 5, glued on one side of it. On one of these sides, that is on the side with the 5-cm strip, another strip of the same width and thickness is nailed, in V-formation, leaving the broad side on the right free. This tool is fixed to the bench. One half-top or the back is placed on the higher part of the 5-cm piece and is held in place with a wedge.

The time has come for the jack plane to enter into action. Of course, its blades are well-sharpened and drawn out just slightly. Beginning from the broader side of wood, you plane in the direction of the grain. With these two tools, you are able to create a perfect and straight grain. Then against the light, you look to see if there are any uneven parts, of all things, so as to ensure that the two ends will form a perfect joint. If you are satisfied with what you see with your eyes, then you have achieved the top joint. Then, with the string, sticks, glue, and wedge, we are ready to start joining the parts together

The most precious and genuine of all the tools for the luthier who makes guitars, bandurias, and lutes is the wood scraper. The usefulness of the wood scraper lies in levelling-off the veneer that has been prepared for the mosaic, and then the strips of wood used for forming the mosaic. With a lot of painstaking care, you will be able to smooth down the veneer to a tenth of a millimeter.

Anyone who has ever seen a guitar being made by a prestigious luthier will realize that these veneers, somewhat black and white in color, with the fine and delicate things you see on the rosette and on the edges of the sound-board, have had to be planed to this hairbreadth thickness with the use of our famous wood scraper. I saw that of the great Santos Hernández, made of wood and undoubtedly by himself. Mine, which I am describing here, was also made of holm oakwood, and is my own creation.

At the workshop where I did my apprenticeship, the woodscraper used a beautiful and ancient iron tool. It is also an extremely useful tool, despite being the first of the dynasty. That of my bosom friend Marcelo Barbero, which I used for two years—he allowed me to use it when I started out and during the time he lived in my house—was made by a mutual family friend named Beltrán, a mechanical fitter who was very skilful. He was the same guy who made Marcelo's bramils. The wood scraper he made was a high-precision tool that was a joy to look at.

As I said, my wood scraper was made by me using holm oakwood from a very used and dry jack plane. It consists of three parts: first, the part that holds the blade; the part that adjusts the blade, letting you plane the right thickness of veneer; and then the part that holds the other two parts firmly and tightly together, serving as a support for the tool. The part holding the blade is cut in the middle (widthways) by 8 cm, and with the aid of two butterfly screws sustains the loose part of the wood and adjusts the blade.

The second part holds a 20-cm wedge, glued in with ductile to prevent it from coming out or sliding along. It is held in place with a screw and a compressed spring, which keep it adjusted to its side while allowing it to slide slightly so that the wedge can get as close as possible to the desired thickness of the cutting blade. This blade will cut the veneer to a decimal size if need be.

The wood scraper is a highly valuable tool for the guitar makers of my time; anyone who made their own mosaic had to use it for hours, even days on end. Imagine for a moment, dear reader, how to reduce by half several hundreds of 40 × 2-cm veneers with thicknesses—and this is really where the challenge lies— of 7 or 8 decimal points of a centimeter. You have to understand that the wood scraper that I am talking about does not *cut* the wood. It only *scrapes* it, stroke after stroke, until it reaches the thickness required by the mosaic and a clearly defined design is obtained.

Just think of the time it takes only to fine-plane the veneer until you get a 10–15 veneered board, depending on the size of the mosaic. This veneer board is only one of the 10 or 15 needed to obtain the drawing of the mosaic chosen. Not only is it time-consuming, but it also requires a lot of patience. More often than not, when you get close to the desired thickness, it breaks, and you have to start all over again. And that is not the end of the story. These little boards must be sawn on one of their sides, again to a thickness of 8/10, and once again, you fine-plane them until you get the perfect square of the veneer that has previously been fine-planed, to 4/10 or 5/10.

Everything is glued together, following the design, to obtain the mosaic that endows the guitar with a personality and identity of its own. This is the case for both classical and flamenco guitars. Let me point out that this adornment, by itself, deserves some kind of admiration. In my opinion, the most illustrious mosaic exponents, on account of their instincts for variation, design, and taste, were Antonio Torres, and Santos Hernández. Torres never repeated a soundhole in his guitars; and Santos was noted for his mosaics, which were always remarkable. Also worth mentioning are the few but excellent guitars constructed by José Ramírez III.

Nowadays, we have more means. And there is no doubt that in this profession, some luthier or an other will construct his own soundholes with their own designs based on his good taste. There will still be others who will have only one design which will be repeated on all their guitars. Yet others will buy prefabricated soundholes on the guitar accessory market.

Well, this is the mission and usefulness of the tool that is so indispensable to us. We also use this tool to fine-plane the veneer for the purfling, top, and back, as well as the back joints

As its name indicates, the electric bending heater bends or "tames" its subject to a desired shape. In our case, to "tame" is to cause the pieces of wood, which we measure for the sides of our guitars, to take the shape of our instrument. The electric bending heater is a 2-mm thick iron tube. The one that I use at present has a power rating of 1,000 watts, and a cover at the upper end that allows me to heat it more or less, to the desired temperature.

I want you to know, dear friend, that the fact that this apparatus is electric is a real luxury. At the workshop where I worked until 1955, and where most of today's luthiers learned their guitar lutherie by following the Madrid school tradition, their burner was fuelled by holm oak charcoal. And I know for certain that our masters before us, Ramírez, Santos, Esteso, Barbero, etc., never used any other system in their guitar-making lives. My nasal sensitivity has a good deal of experience from the countless burners that I lit in my apprentice years.

The guitar sides are then put into a receptacle of the same length, in water (I leave them for several hours) to tame them. Experience in taming this hard wood is very important. Indian Rosewood sides pose few problems, since the grain of this wood is very symmetrical and just a little hard. The great rosewoods from Rio pose a beautiful challenge. Their fantastic grain and wood designs, with their different textures, are gifts of Mother Nature for us to shape into the sides of our guitar. It is not uncommon to find bulges in some parts, and the professionalism of the worker will remedy these anomalies.

Today, it is quite easy to achieve homogeneity in these woods, thanks to the use of guitar-shaped burners, with heat on both sides, which prevent the wood from warping so easily.

The Frets

The little alpaca alloy bars on the guitar's fingerboard are the frets. They create the marvellous polyphony of our guitar.

As everybody well knows, the calculation of the fret measurement and its development, which dates back many centuries, we owe to the great, wise, Greek mathematician Pythagoras (circa 569–475 BC). Much later, the wise

Frenchman, Mersenne, in his *Harmonie Universelle* (París, 1636–37), discussed tuning. However, in between these times, much research on musical temperament was conducted by others.

One of the first pieces of news on the correct annotation of equal temperament took place in China, where the brightest solution by Prince Tsaiyu, still remains an enigma, in view of the fact that Chinese music does not make use of any kind of temperament.

The earlier forms of tuning in equal temperament were devised by Giovanni Maria Lanfranco, in his *Ciencia della Música* (Brescia, 1533). However, it was Mersenne, who in his *Harmonie Universelle*, added and contributed to the acoustics and description of instruments. He expressed equal temperament in numbers, showing the geometry and mechanical solution to tuning. Finally, he put into practice the bases for tuning that are still used today.

Since the second half of the 16th century, theorists have concurred that instruments with frets (lutes, vihuelas, guitars, etc.) have to be tuned with equal temperament. Other evidence is that of the 14th- and 15th-century paintings—in particular those of the meticulous flamenco painters, who were in a class of their own because of the wealth of details of their paintings—in which it can be observed that the frets of the instruments are equidistantly positioned.

At the National Gallery in London, for instance, there are several paintings in which the position of the frets is clearly shown. *El Concierto de Ercole* by Roberti (1450–96) depicts a 9-stringed lute and a small, 4-stringed violin—both apparently in equal temperament. Something similar appears in a work by the painter Marcos Marciales in his *Virgen y niño en el Tronco de Ángeles*, painted between 1493 and 1505. In it you can see an 11-stringed lute with intervals of equal proportions. To give another example, in *El Embajador*, painted by Hans Holbein el Joven (1533), there is a 6-stringed lute with the frets following equal temperament.

The introduction of equal temperament became fashionable with Johann Sebastian Bach, although, as stated above, equal-temperament tuning was already being used many years before him.

Before equal temperament became well-defined, there existed other temperament systems, introduced by Zarlino and Salinas, and known as *igual paratono* (meantone). Possibly the very first and most precise mathematical definition of equal temperament was given by Francisco Salinas in his *De Música Libri VII* (Salamanca, 1577). In it, various former scales were clarified and the remaining imprecise ones were disqualified. Hence, for a lengthy period of time there was no novelty in string vibration knowledge. Not until Galilei (1564–1642) and

Mersenne (1588–1648): these two geniuses, working independently, discovered the time it took a given vibration to go through a length of the string based on its tension, and density. Each note corresponds to a vibration frequency. The harmonic series of the musical notes naturally increases as the frequencies increase, owing to the vibrations in the strings. The frequencies are changed by dividing the open strings into 2 octaves, then 3, 4, 5, 6, and so on. This is equal temperament.

Before Mersenne came Vincenzo Galilei. True, he demonstrated the reason behind the division of the 18th-century scale, since it was the ideal and most convenient to be adapted to the lute.

Of course, simply repeating the use of proportion (18 divisions) does not produce an octave. Many minimal corrections are needed. The frets are arranged horizontally whereas the strings run vertically In a chord, one note will sound in tune whilst another will sound out of tune. A certain interval is appropriate for the musical occasion. And only the ear of the musician playing the instrument will perceive it. Each string vibrates freely in all its extension.

In the classical guitar, the commonest scale in use is 650 mm. Half of that is the octave (the 12th fret), the third part is the 7th fret, and the fourth part is the 5th fret. In the 650 mm string scale, the octave of the 12th fret is 325 mm; the third, or 7th, fret is 216.66 mm; the fourth, or 5th, fret is 162.55 mm. A trial should be made to check that the sound of the different string scales is perceptible to the human ear. Personally, I believe that any ear trained in music can perceive it; especially with our guitar, which has various string scales.

The 63.5-cm scale was used by luthiers prior to Torres, and by composers such as Fernando Sor, Dionisio Aguado, and others.

The scale with the longest experience, and which is mostly used today, is 650 mm. It bears an average weight that acts on the tension of the soundboard, making it possible to use bracings that are not too stiff, and so produce a well-balanced sound between trebles and basses. The 63.5-cm scale, on the other hand, does not give much tautness to the string, and the set of reinforcements on the soundboard may be lighter. As the string is less tight, the guitarist cannot maintain the sound when he wants to pluck the string with a lot of force.

Many years ago I performed an experiment in my Los Angeles workshop, in which I tuned a string with a spring balance. The average weight I obtained was 50 g—the difference in a 63-cm string and a 65-cm string, which is some 3 kg. I was pulling six strings whose lengths varied by a few decimal points. I am sure that with a more precise weighing instrument than my poor spring balance, the calculation would be better than mine and the difference in string scale would be greater than 3 kg. In particular, the longer the string, the greater the tension, whilst the weight will make the string harder to pluck.

The same is true of the sound. The sound of the 65-cm scale is, as I see it, and in my humble experience, the most balanced between the trebles and the basses, and has the most remarkable richness. Do not forget that Antonio Torres was criticized by the Vienna school of guitar for constructing his guitars with a 650-mm string scale. They complained that it was extremely difficult for the ladies of that city to execute certain hand positions.

As I have already affirmed in my previous writings, the 665-mm or 670-mm string scale is an absurdity that many guitar makers, eager to imitate great concert guitarists using their trademark, created and thus limited their own possibilities. It really is difficult to reach certain positions on the fingerboard of a long-stringed guitar; an inconvenience that could easily have been overcome by using much shorter strings.

Fret Division

Since Galileo's division of the temperament scale into 18, many fret divisions have attempted with this system; sometimes the desired string scale is 670 mm, 666.5 mm, 650 mm, and 630 mm. The shortest one should be for classical guitars, and in all likelihood, this was the string scale of the guitars used by the 18th-century composers, as I said earlier on.

But in my opinion, the 650-mm string scale should be the academic scale, the standard scale for both the guitarist and the guitar pedagogue, as well as for the luthier. On the other hand, the quality of the sound produced with the long-scale strings is far from balanced, owing to the fact that longer strings produce more treble sounds. This contributes a guitar's mezzo-soprano sound, and in particular its bass, to the detriment of roundness and deepness.

The fret calculation system I present is a simple and very practical method that my father taught me in my youth. It was the same as the one used by Santos Hernández. As far as I know, Ramírez never used this system in his workshop. What I do know is that Ramírez III built several guitars with different string scales, using the following system: finding the middle of the string scale, the 12th fret, and with the aid of a compass finding 1/18 of the remaining distance. We also had a compensating compass. As the compass opens out, the two tips of the upper side give the 1/18 part of the whole scale. This compass was seldom used. Someone tried sharpening its tips and the proportional distance was lost. A more practical system that has always worked for me starts with first drawing a straight line (a fixed fret calculation can easily be transferred onto the fingerboard of the guitar; besides, this is durable). I recommend an aluminum strip with a thickness of 2 mm and a width of 45 mm, more or less. This straight line must be drawn with a ruler, 5 mm from the edge and 650 mm long. Then, we will design a transversal line (forming a perfect right angle). Taking the two sides that mark out the length, one end will serve as the nut and the other the saddle.

Fingerboard and Bridge

The distance of the fingerboard is multiplied by 1/18: the result is 36.111 mm (this distance can easily be calculated with a digital gauge). Ah, I nearly forgot! With the 650 mm distance you must find the mid-point, which is the 12th fret; then the third part or the 7th fret; and the fourth part, or the 5th fret (if you prefer). These are then carefully marked on the aluminum, in a straight line, with the aid of an awl. Thus we will obtain the nut and the bridge positions, which is the length of the division, then the 5th, 7th, and the 12th frets. With the division of the length into 18 parts at 36.111 mm, and starting from the nut, 36.111 is marked with dotted holes.

The 1/18 part is the width of the angle, which, in a straight line from the bridge, completes the right angle. This width is measured with a fine-tipped compass, from the corner of the angle. Then the remaining frets are measured in a similar manner. The angle marks the correct proportion of the reductions. However, remember that your skillfulness will depend on the precision with which you use the compass. And do not forget that the fixed points for the 5th, 7th, and 12th frets should fall in with what you are about to draw and that each fret in the division must be adjusted to its octave. In other words, the 1st fret with its quarter; the 6th fret with its third of the octave fret, the mid-point of the 13th fret. In this way, each fret has its successive mid point, as well as the third and quarter points. If the above is done with precision, then a perfect fret calculation is an indisputable reality in the temperament scale.

People Who Made Contributions to the Temperamental Tuning System

Pythagoras: (circa 569–475 BC)

Tomás de Santa María: *Arte de tener fantasía* (Valladolid, 1565)

Francisco Salinas: *De Música, Libro VII* (Salamanca, 1577)

Franchinus Gafurius: *Práctica Música* (Milan, 1496)

Vinzenzo Galilei: *Dialogo della Música antica e Moderna* (Florence, 1581)

Claudius Ptolemy: *Harmonicorum Libritres* (London, 1699)

Gioseffo Zarlino: *Dimostrationi Armoniche* (Venice, 1571)

Giovanni Maria Lanfranco: *Scintille de Musica* (Brescia, 1533)

Juan Bermudo: *Declaración de instrumentos musicales* (Ossuna, 1555)

H. L. F. Helmholtz: *Sensation of Tone* (London, 1885)

People in This Century

Murray J. Barbocir: *Tuning & Temperament: A Historical Survey* (New York, 1963)

L. L. S. Lloyd & H. Boyle: *Intervals, Scales & Temperaments* (New York, 1963)

D. Culver Pu and A. Charles: *Musical Acoustic* (New York, 1956)

Theodore Norman: *The Concert Guitar with a Mobile Bridge* (Los Angeles, 1963)

Miguel Ablóniz: *El Diapasón. Guitar News* (1960)

Alex Menarry: *Tuning & Temperaments. Classical Guitar Magazine*, Vol. 12 (August 1994.)

Other Historical Reasons for Equal Temperament and Other Promoters

Outstanding among the 15th-century Spanish theorists was Bartolomé Ramos de Pareja (1440–1525), a professor at the University of Salamanca, who subsequently moved to Bologna, Italy. He fought against the hexachord system, and was all for changing the 4th and the 5th intervals with constant sound. He actually went as far as eliminating the sensitive reality of the "comma" by means of the temperament, which spread these little differences among all the notes of the scale and divided the octave into twelve equal semitones. Even though rejected by the Italians, his system finally prevailed and was the origin of the present one.

At the end of the 15th century, numerous treatises appeared—particular, the rules for the Gregorian chant. The most significant authors were Domingo Marcos Duran (15th–16th C) and Martínez de Bizcargui (15th–16th C), who advocated for the temperament. It was first applied on the guitar, and, shortly afterwards, it spread to keyboard instruments, and in no time at all; it was used generally on every instrument.

3.3. The Tension of the Guitar String; Octave Ccalculation

String Scale

Scale: 660 mm = 66 cm from nut to saddle

660 mm scale: 76 Newtons

Every string: 7.74 kg.

Total: 46.48 kg.

This is the tension of strings in static form. When plucked, on the account of the pressure exerted by the finger, it raises the tension of six strings by 5 kg, while producing a precision scale of 51.48 kg from the bridge to the soundboard.

Another Version

The 65-cm string scale (650 mm) equals 70 Newtons. If 1 kg is 9.82 Newtons, then each string is equivalent to 7.13 kilograms. When fully tightened they add up to 42.8 kg, plus the 5 kgs gained when the strings are plucked = 47.8kg.

Currently, the 65-cm scale is the most commonly accepted and widely used by almost all guitar makers and luthiers.

By striking the difference between the two scales of 660 and 650 mm, you get the following:

660-mm string scale: 51.48 kg.

650-mm string scale: 47.80 kg.

The difference: 3.68 kg.

There is a big difference because the weight in constant tension is significant, since it is the plucking which bears the weight upon contact with the string. The difference, therefore, between the string scale of 650 mm (65 cm) and that of 660 mm (66 cm) is 1 cm.

If we reduced the string scale to 63.5 cm, typical in the days of Sor, Aguado, Lacôte, and in the Viennese, Italian, and Spanish schools, we would obtain the following: 63.5 cm is equal to 60 Newtons in each string, or, if you prefer, 6.11 kg. The six strings will add up to 41.69 kg, which gives a difference of 3.680 kg, with a string scale of 650 mm (+ 5 kg of pressure).

If we increased the string scale to 67.5 cm, as some luthiers do nowadays, we would get 80 Newtons; that is, 8.15 kg in each string, totalling 53. For the soundboard to bear 92 kg with a scale length of 67.5 cm would be extremely inconvenient and painful for the guitarist, who would have to overstretch his fingers in order to reach every position on the fingerboard. In short, you can adopt the following scheme:

63.5-cm string scale: 41.69 kg.

65-cm string scales: 47.81 kg.

66-cm string scale: 51.44 kg.

67.5-cm string scale : 53.92 kg.

Difference:

6 string scale of 5.5 to 65 cm: 3.68 kg.

6 string scale of 5 to 66 cm.: 3.63 kg.

String scale of 66 to 67.5 cm: 2.48 kg.

Another consideration is the shortage of adequate nylon strings that are properly calculated for the different string scales and tension kilos. Frankly speaking, there are neither different string sizes (thicknesses) nor materials to choose from. The ideal thing would be for the guitarist to be able to choose the thickness and type of string that best fits his guitar and sound preferences.

Besides, the vibration undergoes variations owing to the difference that exists between the two pieces extracted from the same trunk. The fiber, hardness, stiffness, and weight are totally different. Since the mechanics and the acoustics of each guitar are distinct, the luthier's experience and technical know-how play a decisive role when it comes to making the right choices of wood to suit the instrument he wants to create. It is almost an intuitive choice, as the luthier cannot determine beforehand the quality and the outcome of the guitar that he is constructing.

"Necessity is the mother of invention." The only way for the guitar maker to obtain the suitable bracings for the soundboard that he is using is to put together all the pieces and frameworks, and to get the correct measurements of the height of the bridge and the scale of the strings over the soundboard and the fingerboard.

If the luthier strictly follows production guidelines, his guitars will probably have a common denominator, even though his instruments will never sound the same. The bitterest pill to swallow in our trade is the impossibility of improving on the sound quantity and quality, as happens with other stringed instruments. In the case of the piano, for instance, you have more possibilities to play with hammers, leather, or felt covers, all of which have different effects. If the hammer dries and hardens up, it produces a hard and colorless sound when it hits the strings. If the cover is made of leather or felt, even when hit hard the sound is quite brilliant. With a leather or felt cover, the sound comes out sweeter and lovelier. If you want a clearer tone, you can reinforce the hammer with another leather or felt cover that is stiffer.

In the violin, the position of the soundpost—a round stick made of old pinewood—is crucial. There is a remarkable difference in clarity, sharpness, and quality depending on its position; that is, depending on how exactly and how vertically it is positioned, and how perfectly it is joined to the top and the back.

None of these improvements can be achieved in our guitar for the simple reason that, once both the nut and the saddle have been adjusted and all the pieces glued together, the sound will be the outcome of its construction, woods, mounting, varnishing, and strings. Absolutely nothing else can be done about it, except that the pressures of the string scale on the soundboard and the bridge will resist to the extent that the mounting and the wood will bear. And the sound and vibrations will be proof of the quality of its construction.

So, only the experience, sensitivity, and intuition of each luthier will enable him to get the most out of his bracings and obtain the instrument he desires.

Calculating the Octave Point:. 12th Fret, 65-cm String Scale

As can be expected, the longer the distance from the 12th fret to the saddle. the more likely it is that the problem of a perfect octave in the sixth string is only partly resolved, owing to the angle formed by the height of the string and the fret on the fingerboard.

By adding 2 mm to the distance between the 12th fret and the bridge, we make up for the prolongation of that part of the string scale. Without this arrangement, the tuning of the guitar and its octave will be imperfect., as the octave is harmonically exact, string by string, in a fret.

With regard to the calculations, we have already established that in the change of distance between strings and the fret, an alteration is called for in the 12th fret, vis-à-vis the bridge and the vibrating parts of the string. The higher the string is from the fingerboard, the bigger the difference between the two parts, between the nut and the 12th fret, and the distance between the octave and the saddle.

The higher the strings, the further the bridge must be moved away from the 12th fret. This calculation is crucial for a perfect tuning. It demonstrates the necessary progression of the "movable bridge"; the fact that each string must have its place on the bridge, in height and length, in relation to each fret, since each string, as we all know, is different in elasticity, thickness, and material. But it is possible to lengthen or shorten the distance of each string within the bridge in order to get perfect octaves in the fingerboard.

Curiosity: Mandolin or Banduria

String scale: 45 cm = 90 Newtons

9.17 kg/string × 12 strings = 110 kg.

Mersenne Laws: *Harmonia Universelle*

The number of vibrations (frequency) per second is:

- Inversely proportional to the length of the string: F = 1/L

- Directly proportional to the square root of the tension of the string: F = Kt

- Inversely proportional to the thickness of the string: f = 1g

- Inversely proportional to the square root of its density: f = 1d

Let :

F = frequency

L = length

t = tension

g = thickness

d = density

Therefore:

L = k/k g

L = k/kt

L = k/kd

g = k/kt

g = k/kd

d = antln (2 ln(k/k)+1/2 ln t)

There are more formulae to relate any variables that you want; for instance, string density and tension. In other words, given a certain tension, we can calculate the density of any string.

Since the guitar is a stringed instrument, it is subject to the laws of tension, thickness, vibration, and pitch; laws discovered by the Franciscan father Père Mersenne and written in his *Harmonie Universelle* (France,

1636). Likewise, they were translated into English by Charles A. Culver PhD (*Musical Acoustics*, 1956).

The laws of vibrations state the following:

1. The number of vibrations per second is inversely proportional throughout the string. The longer the scale of the guitar string, the fewer the vibrations per second.

2. The number of vibrations per second is directly proportional to the square root of the tension of the string. The number of vibrations increases with the tension of the strings. The higher the tension and the higher the pitch, the more vibrations there are and the higher the frequency.

3. The number of vibrations is inversely proportional to the thickness of the string. The thicker the string, the more the vibrations decrease and the lower the frequency.

4. The number of vibrations is inversely proportional to the square root of the density of the string. When the string has higher density in material, the more the vibrations decrease and therefore, the frequency decreases.

Resonance of the Wood Used for Our Guitars

The resonance capacity of the wood depends, naturally, on its physical constitution. The woods that we employ in guitar construction are pine (*Picea abies*, Europe), and Western Red Cedar (*Thuja plicata*, North America), as already stated previously.

The creation of our soundboards is largely influenced by the radial growth of the tree; a direct consequence of itse ring development, temperature, altitude, and climate under which the tree lives. Another determinant is the form of cut: the cut that divides the wood in its natural aperture in the grain. The trunks are cut into four parts, at the double cross. They are then cut into segments, widthwise, to a length a little more than half the width of the soundboard. So, each trunk is cut into four pieces. From each of these pieces you make half of the soundboard, which will be paired up with the next cut. They are then joined together to create the soundboard of the guitar. By joining them together, the center allows you to have the same grain on both sides, producing a totally harmonic board, essential for vibrations and the sound properties of our instrument.

The funny thing is that, when you cut a useful trunk into segments, the symmetry of a piece with its subsequent pair does not exist, owing to the fiber, orientation, and growth of the tree.

The density, like the weight, varies considerably at different parts of the trunk. The difference is due to the oscillations in growth of the tree, during the spring and summer periods. For this reason, in the summer, the wood is two-and-a-half times as dense and hard as the circular grain of the trunk felled in the spring, which is lighter in color.

The pine's narrow grain, with a marked hard circle, is relatively dense in the summer. The wood is denser and harder when the circle is thicker.

It is very common among experts well-versed in forestry to affirm that the location of a tree on a mountain and the bio-chemical composition of its soil affect not only the density of the wood, but also the acoustic properties of that musical instrument.

According to the laws of wood resonance by Franz Jahnel (*Manual de Tecnología de la guitarra*) the lower the gravity, the higher the note; the lower the wood elasticity, the higher the vibration frequency; and the lower the hardness-smoothness, the lower the frequency.

The consequence is therefore that the guitar soundbourd must be light in weight and absolutely smooth.

The weight is also influenced by the drying process of the wood, its elasticity, and the sameness of the grain. All these properties are relative values, taking into account what has been said before: the difference in the various parts of the trunk.

Every soundboard is an unknown in itself, and its outcome depends only on the skill, knowledge, and experience of the luthier who is constructing the instrument.

The resonance capacity of the wood depends on its physical nature. As with metals, if wood is cut into two pieces of equal length, width, and thickness, and both are hung on one of the sides, then when struck with a blunt object, the sound they produce will be identical as far quality and vibration are concerned.

Reflection of Sound

There are two types of sound reflections: diffuse and regular. The sound is *diffuse* when the surface at which it is reflected is uneven. By contrast, it is *regular* when the surface at which it is reflected is clean, bright, and uniform.

If the sound waves reflect against a uniform surface, the reflection thus produced will be maximized. If they are reflected against an elastic or irregular material, such as soft wood, absorption occurs.

Following the theory of Steinweg and Brosnac on the forms of vibration on pine soundboard, picture 1 is an example of a correct vibration. Picture 2 is an example of an incorrect vibration .

To my way of seeing things, the correct vibration of the soundboard in picture 1 is due to the fact that it has an in-built bracing design which counter-reacts against the pressure which, in this case, the soundboard must be able to bear. Picture 2 is a wooden soundboard without any bracings at all, whereby the vibrations are lost. This is a glaring example of how the stiffness of the wood is a determining factor. The soundboard reinforced with bracings is much stiffer than the one that has no such support.

3.4. Typical Bracings

Inside the Guitar

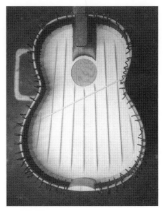

One of my experiments.
Los Angeles, 1963.

The guitar luthier does not have the chance to vary the structure while at the same time get the instrument to produce sound. Only the inquisitive man—thanks to his curiosity and love for the instrument he creates—wishes to know the whole range of probabilities within his reach in order to obtain the ideal guitar. For this reason, this professional feels the need to carry out experiments. "Every movement, whatever its cause may be, is always a creative movement."

The guitar is, as you play it, the instrument that is closest to the body. In its design, it also has the likeness of the human body. It is, perhaps, the most romantic of all the musical instruments.

In honor of this sentiment, the guitar maker needs to create something better and different from everything he has previously made. Hence, the true professional is the one who, out of his curiosity, creates his guitar and signs it as the best instrument possible with the optimum sound he is capable of. The professional always experiments. He needs to know to believe in what he does.

Here are some designs by some past luthiers and copies of my own notes about the construction specifications of my guitars. I am also including several examples of bracing designs extracted from my notebook, indicating the dates on which my guitars were made.

In the catalogue that we currently publish, both the handcrafted guitars—100% handmade with choice matured wood—and those manufactured on the production line—70% handmade—we feature bracing designs ranging from the simplest guitars to the ones made with my own hands.

My Bracing Experiment in Los Angeles (1963)

The film depicts the third-generation guitar maker, Manuel Rodríguez, constructing a fine guitar from imported woods, and using the tools that his family used for three generations. From the selection of the wood we see the shaving, chiselling, sawing, and forming of a fine guitar much in the same way it has been done for centuries; the meticulous craftsmanship juxtaposed

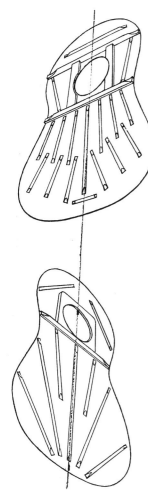

Types of bracing, used in many publications.

with the quick editing cuts of motion pictures of some of the great accomplishments of guitar making. The implication, of course, is that the attention to detail, integrity, and commitment are those things that allow man to reach greatness.

With these calculations, we can say that these are the bracings, so different and anarchical, that the soundboard must have, without it stopping the strings from producing a sustained quality pitch sound.

Allow me to express my most heartfelt homage, in my capacity as a luthier, to all guitar pedagogues and concert guitarists from every corner of this planet for their contributions to the teaching of our instrument. With their dedication and enthusiasm, they have contributed immensely to the satisfaction of their disciples and families, and that of their audiences, who delight in their concerts or buy printed music.

In my youthful years, in the 1940s, the teachers in Madrid were La Fuente, Esquembre Moreno, the Hererro family, Regino Sainz de la Maza and his brother Eduardo, Daniel Fortea, and other distinguished teachers.

Current Bracings: Bracing Inside the Soundboard; Precursors: Antonio Torres and Other Luthiers.

As can be observed in *La guitarra Española*, certain guitar makers from the south of Spain ventured to put some strips of wood as bracing inside the soundboard, beneath the bridge, behind the stick, and after the soundhole.

José de Frías (1777)

In his precious guitar, its soundboard appears decorated with a mother-of-pearl and ebony filigree. Inside the soundboard, and on both sides of the space of the bridge, there are two bracings.

Juan Pagés (Cádiz, 1792)

This man, who hailed from the same town as my father, seems to have been more imaginative than the above-mentioned. Inside his soundboard, he glued five bracings covering the bridge, three in line with the grain and two in the corner forming the angle. In addition, it has two transversal sticks at the sides of the soundhole. But the novelty was that at both sides of the soundhole he stuck three bracings, and, at the top part of the bar, another three crossed bracings.

José Benedid (Cádiz, 1794)

More modest than his colleagues', his guitar has three bracings parallel with the grain under the bridge.

José Martínez (Málaga, 1792)

This guitar has seven bracings under the soundboard. The bracings are of no particular significance, as they must have been glued in during two repair works.

Agustín Caro (Granada, 1803)

A watch repairer turned guitar maker, he fitted five bracings under the bridge, parallel to the soundboard.

Salvador Pau (Valencia, 1830)

His bracing consists of five sticks and two strips on the soundhole, transversal sticks, and three bracings at the back. I am afraid this guitar was repaired.

In Andulusia, bracings were beginning to be used inside the soundboard; in Madrid, the idea was not even considered.

Benito Sánchez de Aguilera (Madrid, 1797)
Manuel Muñoa (Madrid, 1804)
Manuel Narciso Gonzales (Madrid, 1833)

None of these luthiers constructed their guitars with bracings inside and under the bridge. Probably Maestro Aguado influenced Muñoz and Juan Moreno to reinforce the inside of their soundboards.

We have on record a guitar made by Muñoz in 1807 with three bracings and three transversal sticks in the back. We also have guitars by Juan Moreno: one constructed in 1829 and another in 1830. The former was made following the traditional style, whereas the latter had modern features.

It seems historical that these breakthroughs in the development of bracing are those that helped Maestro Antonio Torres to establish the final form of the soundboard bracing of the Spanish guitar.

Researching in the gallery of fine guitars in *Guitar Reviews No. 30*, I discovered the following:

> • A Venetian guitar. The fingerboard and the soundboard form a joint. This is the 10-fret guitar guitar of Rizzio, belonging to Queen Mary of Scotland. Damper model of 1561.

> • Guitars made in Italy and Austria between 1600–1700 were still being constructed with the 10th fret passing over the top-neck joint and inside the wood of the soundboard.

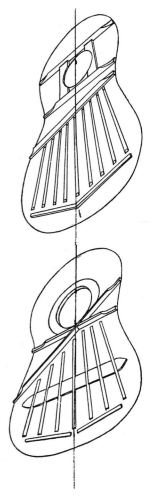

Types of bracing, used in many publications.

Model C3-C1 Abeto
Bracing Pattern

Model E Bracing Pattern

Model CUTWAY
Bracing Pattern

Model Norman
Bracing Pattern

Model Manuel JR.
Bracing Pattern

In Spain the following are worthy of note:

José Massague (Barcelona, 1750)

Its fingerboard is on the same level as the soundboard, and it has 19 frets. It has a soundboard-neck joint.

José Frías (Sevilla, 1777)

As in the previous one, the fingerboard is on the same level as the soundboard. The 10th fret is on the neck-soundboard joint.

Francisco Saguiño (Sevilla, 1759)

A guitar that seems to be cut at the neck. The frets end at the neck and the soundboard joint. Hence there are only nine frets.

Lorenzo Alonso (Madrid, 1786)

The ebony fingerboard is on the same level as the soundboard with eleven frets of plain metal. The 10th fret is on the neck-soundboard joint.

Juan Pagés (Cádiz, 1792)

The fingerboard is on the same level as the soundboard, with equidistant frets, (eleven) and top-soundboard joint.

José Martínez (Málaga, 1792)

The fingerboard is on the same level as the soundboard, which has sixteen metallic frets, four of which are located on the soundboard. The 12th fret is therefore at the point where the neck joins the body of the guitar.

José Martínez was a highly regarded guitar maker in his day; Sor even mentioned his name in his method for the guitar. He eventually constructed a guitar with the 12th fret of the octave on the soundboard and the neck joint.

Benito Sánchez Aguilera (Madrid, 1797)

The fingerboard is on the same level as the soundboard; the 12th fret is on the neck-soundboard joint. He was the first Madrilenian guitar maker to put the 12th fret as the octave, as is the order of the day in classical and flamenco guitars today.

Taking the two guitars, constructed in 1680, and featured in issue No.10 of *Guitar Review* as a reference, we observe that the 12th fret (the octave) is exactly on the neck-soundboard joint

According to Thomas T. Heck in his book, *El nacimiento de la guitarra clásica y su florecimiento en Viena*, before 1700, there was a major contribution to guitar construction from Italy. Certain guitars began to be constructed with necks that had the total octave in the string scale, and the 12th fret was inlaid at the level where the fingerboard joins the soundboard.

The great violin maker Antonio Stradivari could well have been the author of this innovation as found in those guitars that bore his name (1680). But we must remember that the 18th fret was not in Italian music nomenclature. Stradivari, at that time, must have considered this problem, and must have adopted the perspective of the luthier who was interested in perfection; and bypassed the previous standards.

Well, this is all that Dr. Heck has to say about the matter. Actually, throughout his life, Stradivari constructed only four guitars. The genius is born and made, as shown by guitar No. 30 in the gallery of ancient instruments. It is a guitar with five double strings and worms, with 18 frets at the soundboard-neck joint, and the fingerboard level with the soundboard. The 6 other frets are incrusted in the soundboard.

On the soundboard-fingerboard joint there is an emblem of a noble family (it seems to be that of the person who constructed it). And on the back of the headstock you can read the inscription "A. Stradivarius Cremonen S.F. 1680." This magnificent guitar belongs to the collection of W. E. Hill and Sons of London.

In issues 30 and 32 of the magazine, out of the 52 guitars from the 15th, 16th, and 17th centuries, only those made by Stradivari, and another made by the French luthier Alexandre Voboam (Paris, 1690) have six strings. The latter is a lovely guitar, with the 12th fret on the soundboard-neck joint and a string scale length of 61.4 cm. In Dr. Heck's view, this is the ideal guitar.

3.5. My Movable Bridge (Los Angeles, 1960–1961)

In the first year of our happy arrival in the United States, in the city of Los Angeles to be precise, my bosom friend and the person behind my relocation—the remarkable violinist and lecturer at the University of Los Angeles, Theodore Norman—told me about his constant experiments in the quest for the optimum tuning of the guitar.

A violin professor with the Los Angeles Symphony since its beginning, a musician and composer of the great school and a disciple of eminent masters, his tuning as a violist was perfect. Mr. Norman shared his concern with me and asked me about the possibility of correcting the rigid temperament tuning in the guitar. With fixed frets that are transversal to the strings, and are the same for the six strings, there is practically no possibility of making up for any errors. The nut has so narrow a size (54 mm) that there is practically no adjustment possible to effect any significant corrections. The only feasible adjustments can be done on the saddle.

So I divided the bridge into six slots, one for each string. I incrusted these "mini" bridges in the form of angles, in descending order. This prevents them from sliding along with the strings and therefore makes it impossible for the strings to come out. Besides, it offers the possibility of adjusting the strings on the top of the bridge without any vibrations or movements that may cause string buzzing. With these six "mini" bridges, one for each string and moving in line with the strings, the string scale can be lengthened or shortened. Prolongation of the string scale is a usual practice in the modern guitar, where extra distance is added to the basses to make up for the height of the strings on the fingerboard. As the bass string is pressed, the tone increases, unlike in the case of the trebles, which are closer to the fingerboard and have less angle as they are pressed down.

With these six bridges and prolonged string scale, first the height difference between the basses and treble is adjusted, then you obtain unison in the chords. For the guitarist, this is the only practical possibility of achieving a tuning that is in keeping with his own demands.

The idea of dividing the guitar bridge saddle into segments also reminded me that, in the '40s, when groups of serenaders were in hot demand, those musicians encountered the same tuning problems in their instruments.

In those years, Granada was not as much a place for guitarists as it is today. The vast majority of those musicians got their supply of guitars from Madrid guitar makers.

I got to know several of them. One of those banduria players knew that I was making bandurias at night, after working with Ramírez during the day.

He knew perfectly well the groups of serenaders that then existed in Madrid. For instance, the Aragón company; the Estándar Electric group, conducted by my unforgettable friend José Ibañez; and the Albeceta Choir and Serenaders. These serenaders' groups thrived in Madrid, as did the magnificent Orquesta Ibérica, made up of plucking-and-plectrum instruments, and conducted by Maestro J. Lagos.

Well, to come back to the banduria player whose name I do not remember: he intimated to me his concern about tuning, and I made him a bone saddle that could be moved according to the whim and caprice of the musician. Just by adjusting it, he could tune the treble and the bass strings.

I constructed quite a number of guitars with this kind of bridge throughout my stay in Los Angeles. The first one I made was for my personal use. Today, I make them on demand for guitarists concerned about tuning their guitars to achieve maximum perfection: professors from Sweden, Finland, England, and the USA.

I would like to clarify something here. In the years I lived in Los Angeles, the only thing I was able to do was devote all my time to constructing my guitars. When I later became involved with the musical world around me, I realized that the electric guitar already had a bridge where each movable metal string can be adjusted by screws.

I do not really know whether that bridge was before or after mine. What I do know is that the reason behind its construction is the same. The only difference, however, is that the steel string is much more balanced, with less propensity for going out of tune. Again, the guitarist has a whole range of string thickness to choose from, depending on his taste and tuning preferences. This only goes to prove that the strings of an electric guitar are better to tune than those of the classical guitar, for which one can only use one type of nylon string, and that type can get stretched out.

With a movable bridge, in which each string can be adjusted to the frets, you can achieve well-tuned octaves and chords in optimum intonation.

"Whether you like it or not, the individual musical interval is approved insofar as it is determined by the ear of the musician" (L. L. S. Lloyd).

"No true idea in harmony is based on equal temperament." (Sir Donald Tovey, Encyclopedia Britannica, Harmony section).

Guitar Constructed by Beniot Sanchez Alguilera. Madrid, 1797

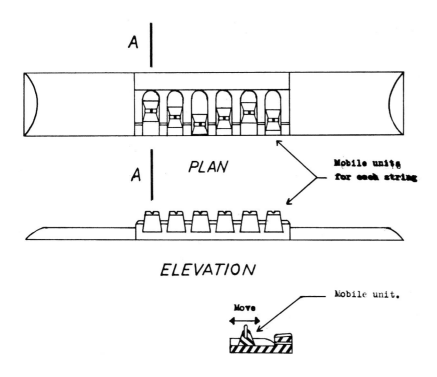

A

PLAN

A

Mobile units for each string

ELEVATION

Move   Mobile unit.

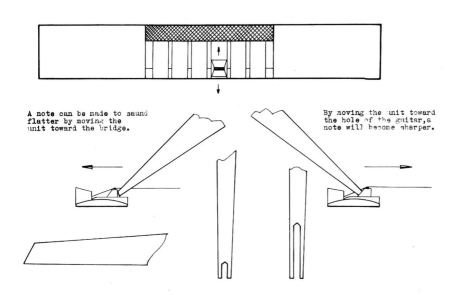

A note can be made to sound flatter by moving the unit toward the bridge.

By moving the unit toward the hole of the guitar, a note will become sharper.

My Mobile Bridge
Los Angeles 1963

Chapter 4

Exhibitions and Schools

La guitarra
hace llorar a los sueños.
El sollozo de las almas
perdidas,
se escapa por su boca
redonda.
Y como la tarántula
teje una gran estrella
para cazar suspiros,
que flotan en su negro
aljibe de madera.

FEDERICO GARCÍA LORCA

4.1. Frankfurt Fair (1983)

In the winter of 1981–82, from December to January, the Arts and Craft Exhibition of the province of Madrid was held. It was organized by the Provincial Craftsmen Association and sponsored by the Madrid City Council and its Culture Department.

The Craftsmen Association sent out invitations asking all the guitar luthiers of Madrid to participate; so a meeting was held in this office of this organization. It was my first contact with these colleagues of mine since my return to Madrid in 1973. I met some of them for the very first time. It was the right time for us to get to know each other and start fraternizing.

We exhibited our guitars in the pavilion and some speeches were made. Almost all the guitar makers of Madrid were present. Only those who did not believe in the fellowship of the guild did not show up; for their absence could not be attributed to financial reasons, as we did not have to foot any financial costs whatsoever.

In the summer of the same year, the National Arts and Crafts Fair was organized. The Chamber of Commerce invited us, and we exhibited our guitars in a flashy pavilion. On this occasion, only eight of us participated.

Over the course of the fair, the representative of the Frankfurt Fair organization visited us. On meeting us, this kind lady invited us, the Madrid School guitar craftsmen, to exhibit our guitars in a show, and stand under the name "Guitar Craftsmen. Madrid School." We set to work. We applied for a stand and for the corresponding subsidy from the INFE (the export promotion organization), which was granted. We rented handcraft-related decorations and had them transported from Madrid. On the day before the fair, we went to have a look at our stand. We found the spacious pavilion completely

The artists

The artists and their sons

Our stand at the Frankfurt Fair

empty—our consignment had been held up at the fair's customs. We had to pay the price for our inexperience. During the night, the truck arrived with our consignment. As we were proactive men, we worked until late and the stand was ready for the inauguration of the fair the following morning. I believe it was a very good attraction for the public and for the rest of the music industry. It was typically Spanish: each craftsman was present with his guitars in an area to himself, with his labels, pictures of his workshop, typical tables and chairs, rustic furniture, lamps, and the additional incentive of being the never-seen-before attraction in any music fair. We even had three big barrels of very good wine.

With our guitars and the good wine, which elevated the spirits of those who visited us, we made that fair a memorable and pleasurable experience for some of us.

Sincerely, I think the fact that there were eight craftsmen dedicated to the construction of the same instrument, from the same city, and competing for the same customers, posed a great challenge. If you consider the eight of us, although we were luthiers of the same instrument, there were differences between us—the richness is in the diversity of criteria, our presentations and the individual quality of our guitars. As such, anyone who wanted to try them could get a feel of those different qualities and find out for himself what he most wanted from a guitar and choose accordingly.

This choice factor is the true value of the Madrid school: anyone who wants the best in a guitar can choose from among these instruments. Madrid is the only city on the planet that offers this wide-ranging choice of guitars.

4.2. Madrid Guitar Luthier School

Their Biographies; Exhibitors at the Frankfurt Musical Fair (February 1983)

Vicente Camacho

A native of Madrid and the son of a cabinetmaker, he learned the trade from his father. His hobby, music, led him to take part in serenaders' troupes and other musical groups. Thus he met his future master, Modesto Borreguero, who was the workmate of Santos Hernández and Domingo Esteso at the Manuel Ramírez workshop.

He worked with Borreguero for eight years and was the only handyman this master had.

He set up his own workshop, working for Madrid, Barcelona, and subsequently for the whole world.

Felix Manzanero

Born in Madrid in 1937, at 14 he entered the José Ramírez workshop as an apprentice, where he learned the rather difficult craft of making stringed instruments. After 14 years, he opened his own workshop on Santa Ana Street, where the best concert guitarists from all over the world have passed by to admire his guitars.

For some years now, he has dedicated most of his time to guitar research. He has been able to finish a guitar without a fan bracing and with a seventh string within it. He has also constructed an elliptic guitar with the aim of endowing it with more sound power. Currently, he is undertaking research in collaboration with another engineering team on the development of an apparatus capable of reading the optimum measurement of the soundboard before it is fitted on the instrument.

Felix Manzanero possesses a large collection of veteran guitars from around the world. It is worth the admiration of every guitar collector. His collection is exhibited at his shop-workshop alongside his research findings.

Paulino Bernabé

Paulino Bernabé was born in Madrid in July 1932. At 17, he studied classical guitar under Maestro Daniel Fuertes for four years. At 22, he went to work for José Ramírez as his helper, and ended up in charge of the workshop in 1969.

"My true work as an independent guitar maker started from that time onwards. I was 38 then, and I set up my workshop at 8 Cuchillero Street, near the Plaza Mayor, Madrid. Breaking off with my guitar past, I created a new way of making the inner structure of the guitar, which brought me a lot of success.

"Since 1973, the great concert guitarist Narciso Yepes, along with many others of universal renown, has been playing 10-stringed guitars made by me. In 1974, I was awarded the Gold Medal at the International Craft Fair held in Munich (Germany).

"For some years now, my workshop has been protected, as I have been granted a little official subsidy through the Gremio Artesanias Varias; my research work on every aspect of the guitar being considered valuable."

Manuel Contreras

"I was born in Madrid, and most of my life has been spent at my workshop making guitars, always in pursuit of the secret of the guitar and endeavouring to enhance its sound.

"I began constructing guitars (my former trade was cabinetmaking) at the José Ramírez workshop in 1959, as first handyman. In 1962, I opened my own workshop at 80 Mayor Street, where I still am.

"Without going into much detail (owing to lack of space), I would like to say that, four years ago, with a technique quite different from those traditionally used, I started constructing guitars with double soundboards; so much so, that currently all my guitars are made with this system.

"I can also say and prove (although it may sound like boasting) that in all my 24 years as a luthier, I have made guitars for nearly all the most famous concert guitarists in the world. In 1979, I was awarded the Export Prize by the Madrid Chamber of Commerce and Industry. In 1980, the same Chamber of Commerce gave me an honorable mention—the first and the only time these prizes have been awarded to a craftsman."

Luis Arostegui Granados

Born in 1932, at 20 he began to make guitars, bandurias, and lutes under the best masters of his time. His guitars are exported to the whole world, and receive praise from all his customers.

Marcelino López

Marcelino López was born in 1931. He studied music and classical guitar under Maestro Daniel Fortea for six years.

In 1984, he started making guitars as a hobby, and took to the luthier profession as a vocation. He also works in the bowed stringed instrument group: viols, viola da braccio, viola da gamba, etc; and bygone keyboard instruments: virginals, clavichords, five-octave fortepianos, etc.

Currently, he makes a series of ornamented baroque instruments.

He received the first prize at the International Ronda Competition in 1979, and his comprehensive luthier art is known all over the world.

Juan Álvarez Gil

Juan Álvarez Gil was born in Madrid in 1932. He constructed his guitars as a hobby, in 1946, together with his brother Lorenzo. He subsequently met Don Marcelo Barbero, a great guitar maker, who taught him the secrets of guitar construction. From then onwards, he felt great curiosity for his work.

His guitars are used by professionals the world over.

His sons, Juan Miguel and Antonio, aged 22 and 19 respectively, have followed their father's footsteps in the guitar construction tradition.

Manuel Rodríguez

"I was born in Madrid. My father was a guitar maker who started at the old workshops that existed in Madrid at the end of the past century.

"At 13, I started learning the craft—and art—of making guitars at the same workshop where my father was working. My guitars, handmade and signed by me, date as far back as 1945.

"Today, my guitars are my dedication and personal art, and I expect my children to take after me."

Jose Romanillos

Jose Romanillos, a cabinetmaker by profession, was born in Madrid in 1932. He went to England in 1956, and made his first guitar five years later. A meeting with Julian Bream led him to take up guitar making professionally in 1970.

4.3. Other Luthier Guitar Schools in Granada, Barcelona, Valencia

The guitar is the most genuinely Spanish musical instrument in the history of Spain. Naturally, it was constructed in many regions, but mainly in Andalusia and the Levante region, where it was heavily influenced by the civilization of the Mare Nostrum coasts—our own Mediterranean Sea. In Andalusia, Granada was the foremost city in this respect.

In the chronicles and regulations concerning the wood trade, one could easily include the vihuela maker, meaning that the vihuela maker would be listed along with the carpenters, cabinetmakers, and church sculptors, since he was the one who made and repaired harps, bowed stringed instruments, clavichords, vihuelas, and lutes.

If my understanding of the regulations governing these trades is right, these craftsmen must have been the best copyists—judging from their results. They improved both furniture and musical instruments. It is evident that the results of their labor are marvellous, considering that some of them have survived up to the present day.

The regulations of these lords of Granada date from 1528, after the Reconquista, which makes us suppose that these trades may have originated from Arab craftsmen. But all this information was lost in history, and so the first record of a guitar appears in 1792: it was in the town of Baza, and the guitar belonged to Rafael Vallejo, expert in ornamentation.

Another superb Granada guitar, dated 1829, was constructed by Agustín Cano, a craftsman who is said to have built his guitars in his free time, since he was otherwise in a different trade.

Granada stands out for its numerous craftsman trades; the main wood trades are the marquetry of wood, bone, and other materials. They make beautiful cabinets and sideboards. It is therefore natural to include in these wood-craftsman trades the construction of furniture, guitars, and other Andalusian popular folklore instruments, such as bandurrias, lutes, and percussion.

Domingo Prat makes mention of Antonio Llorente (1832) in his dictionary, and gives the following description: "Intelligent guitar constructor, said to know a guitar and use the best of woods."

This brings us to José Pernas, in 1850, from whom Antonio Torres is believed to have learned the guitar-making trade. José Pernas must have been one of the authentic guitar luthier pioneers, giving his full-time dedication to guitar making. He is known to have constructed various styles of guitars with significant innovations. Antonio Torres was no doubt infected by José Pernas's curiosity and yearning for the enhancement of our guitar.

The Granada guitar makers who followed, as from the last years of the 19th century, emulated Torres's construction model. One of them was Antonio Valle, son of Agustín Valle and brother of Nicholás Valle, according to the label on his instruments, 1877. Another was José Ortega, guitar maker, who is said to have taught Benito Ferrer the art of guitar making .

Benito Ferrer

Benito Ferrer is undoubtedly the founder of the present day guitar-making school of Granada. He set up shop in 1875, and changed his address on several occasions before his death in August 1925. He was succeeded by his nephew, Eduardo Ferrer, who was born in Granada in 1905. Like the Madrid guitar makers of his days, he suffered the typical vicissitudes of the period: the hardships of the war. He taught his son José the trade, together with most of the guitar makers who are well-established in Granada today. His construction scheme was a replica of that of Antonio Torres.

Currently, the Granada guitar makers follow the models and templates of the Madrid guitar luthier school, such as Ramírez, Santos Hernández, Esteso, and Barbero; with the exception of one who adopted the construction model of a French luthier, who in turn had learned from the Madrid guitar makers and whom I met personally.

Benito Ferrer's Followers

José Ferrer: Benito Ferrer's son who, like me was born in 1926.

Miguel Robles: He was born in Granada in 1902. Maestro of the Taracea, he became a guitar maker at Ferrer's. He worked with Ramírez II before the Civil War, doing those difficult tasks required in banduria making. Miguel Robles worked with me at José Ramírez's in the late 1940s. I have a group photograph of all those of us who worked in that workshop at the time. I remember him as a friend. He was a good companion in those difficult years. He was not with us for very long, since he had left his family in Granada and was unable to bear the separation.

J. L. Bellido: Born in 1943, he worked with Ferrer and married one of his daughters.

M. López Bellido: A cabinetmaker from the age 13, he came to work at the workshop in Ferrer's house when he finished his military service. He was born in Granada in 1933.

Manuel de la Chica: He was born in Granada in 1911. He began—as did most guitar makers of those days— in the cabinetmaking trade. When he was 30, he became a guitar maker. He created his guitars with the construction models of the Madrilenian Santos Hernández and his emulator Marcelo Barbero. I met him during a visit he paid to Madrid in the late 1950s. Today, he is retired in Granada, his home town.

F. Manuel Díaz: He was born in Granada in 1943. He started at Ferrer's and then he worked with M. de la Chica, of whom he considers himself to be a disciple.

Miguel López Muñoz: He was born in Granada in 1939. A cabinetmaker by profession, he became a guitar maker under the management and coaching of Benito Ferrer, whose ways and advice he followed.

Martín Montero: He was born in Granada in 1933. At 20, he was an apprentice cabinetmaker, then he entered Eduardo Ferrer's workshop, where he learned our trade.

Manuel Martínez de Milán: He was born in Granada in 1923. He, too, was a cabinetmaker to start with, and learned the guitar-making trade from Benito Ferrer. He was in Madrid in the mid '50s. His guitar-making skills were not very brilliant; but during his stay in Madrid, he learned a lot from Marcelo Barbero, whom he often visited and even did some repairs for. I got to know him quite well from these visits to Marcelo's. He established himself on Rodas Street. His speed at making guitars allowed him to obtain good prices from flamenco professionals who were not too demanding. His bohemian lifestyle made his workshop more than a mere guitar-making workplace. He soon disappeared from the trade, deserting his wife and two children. His son, who bears the same name, is a guitar maker of good professional standing, but regrettably, is not in guitar making. He lives in Granada with his family and works in another sector.

B. Milán Suárez: Another handyman from the Ferrer's workshop, who dated his guitar in 1899.

Rafael M. Rodríguez: He was born in 1954. He worked in Ferrer's workshop under the management of Eduardo Ferrer until he got established on his own.

G. Pérez Barranco: Granada, 1940. On finishing his military service, he worked with E. Ferrer and M. de la Chica.

A. Raya Pardo: Born in Jaén, 1950. He was a follower of Ferrer through J. L. Bellido.

A. Reinosa: He was born in Granada in 1954. At 13, he started working at E. Ferrer's workshop and then continued with A. Durán.

Luis Arostegui Granados: Born in Granada in 1932, he was the son of a cabinetmaker. After many years in this trade, he switched to guitar making through the influence of Manuel de la Chica, whom he had observed at work. He came to Madrid in 1970, and joined those of us who exhibited at the Frankfurt Fair in 1982. He is still in Madrid, in his workshop at Chueca Plaza.

Rafael Díaz: Granada, 1941. After working at various trades, he found his ideal position in guitar making. He works with his brother Francisco in the workshop jointly owned by both.

Antonio Durán: Granada, 1940. He started off as a cabinetmaker, and worked in other trades. He passed through the Ferrer workshop, making castanets at the beginning and becoming a real expert at it. Today, he manages his own workshop and designs his guitars himself.

Antonio Ariza: Born in Granada in 1939. He, too, was a cabinetmaker in his youth. He passed through the Ferrer workshop, where he learned the guitar-making trade. He is Santos Hernández's follower.

Francisco Fernández: Born in Baza (Granada) in 1930, he is M. Martínez de Milán's brother-in-law and disciple. He ran the workshop on Rodas street in Madrid after the maestro left.

J. Román Padilla: Granada, 1928. Cabinetmaker who must have learned from E. Ferrer and M. de la Chica.

A. Rosales López: Granada, 1928.

F. Santiago Marín: Granada, 1946. A professional cabinetmaker, he is Antonio Marín's nephew, who taught him the trade.

Other disciples of Ferrer were José Castaño, Isidro Garrido, and J.L. Aguilarte.

The above-mentioned people are from the Guitar Making Guild of Granada. It is possible that there are more members today. Welcome! (Good note should be taken of how the Ferrer family produced numerous disciples. The Ramírez family of Madrid did not produce that many disciples. At any rate, only a few in both cases were born guitar makers; rather they were apprentices during the early stages of their professional careers. Most of them were cabinetmakers before becoming guitar makers.)

Valencian Guitar Makers

Andrés Marín: His guitars were very popular. His sons continued with their father's trade, but they disappeared from the scene soon before the Civil War.

Salvador Ibáñez: Another pioneer in guitar manufacturing in Valencia. He died in 1920. His sons followed him, but they also died in the Civil War.

Telesforo Julve: Yet another prestigious and productive guitar manufacturer from the Valencia region. He had a good market in the Hispanic world, but must have lost it in the 1960s with the advent of the Japanese guitar.

Telesforo Julve stood out in the 1940s, and continued manufacturing for some more years.

Valencia and Its Guitar Construction Industry

In the history of Valencia, there has been no known guitar luthier. There must have been in centuries past, but I have not found any information on them.

The history of the guitar's construction begins in the first decades of the 20th century with names such as Marín, Telesforo Julve, Vicente Tatay (and later his sons), Ricardo and Vicente Sanchis Badia, and others.

Several guitars we repaired in the 1940s had been made by Marín.

Currently, one of the most veteran workshops is that of Ricardo Sanchis, which was founded in 1915 in Masanasa (Valencia). It is managed today by his son Vicente Sanchis Badia. I got to know these guitars, bandurias, and lutes on Carretas Street in Madrid during my youth in the 1940s. In those days, these instruments were constructed with wooden pegs; the mechanical peg box was optional. Given that my "barber" (Barbero) did the repair jobs for this workshop, he would hand over the task of fixing the peg boxes to me, so that I would do it with my good old brace, gimlet, and pointed handsaw that I used for making grooves. This is why I am so familiar with them. Without any doubt, those instruments were among the best manufactured in Valencia. Today, their construction, judging from advertisements made by the firm, is guaranteed by "81 years of top-quality craftsmanship."

Vicente Tatay and Sons

According to the information I have, this firm was established in the 1920s. It was formed by Don Vicente and his sons and later carried on by relatives and other workmen. It is said that Tatay Sr. came to Madrid and offered to supply José Ramírez II with student guitars. This was an answer to Ramírez's prayer, as he was never particularly hopeful about the workmen of his own workshop. This factory, therefore, supplied Ramírez with these guitars—which were constructed with pegs—and bandurias and lutes. In my youth, I got to fix a good many of those peg boxes.

Guitarras Enrique Keller S. A. (Zarauz, Guipúzcoa)

This factory, without counting the central and Levante areas, is the biggest in Spain; both in terms of guitar production and the number of workmen.

It was founded by Don Enrique Séller, who arrived from his native Germany in 1944. It is a very high-production shop, manufacturing everything from beginners' models all the way up to concert guitars. His construction style is basically his own, following the German model.

In Valencia

After the 1950s, new factories were created in Valencia—today they are the oldest ones—with workmen who become emancipated and created their own models. These are:

Guitarras Prudencio Sáez: currently called Guisama S.L. Torrente (Valencia). It has a workforce of 33 who are quality-oriented in the production of every one of their guitar models. They exhibit at international fairs. The factory was founded in 1963.

Raimundo y Aparicio (Paterna, Valencia).

Ricardo Sanchis Carpio (Valencia).

Vicente Tatay Badia (Masanasa, Valencia).

Vicente Tatay Tomás (Valencia).

Amalio Burquet (Cataroja, Valencia).

Guitarras Azahar (Aldaya, Valencia).

Guitarras Francisco Estevez (Alvoraya, Valencia).

Guitarras Mervi (San Antonio de Benagever, Valencia).

Guitarras Miguel Ángel (Foyos, Valencia).

José Tatay Cuenca (Valencia).

In Barcelona

In Barcelona, as in Madrid, there were eminent craftsmen who towered over others. At present, they work as great luthiers. Some of them are:

Enrique García: Born in Madrid in 1868. The son of another guitar maker, Juan García, he followed his father's trade and became a maestro in Manuel Ramírez's workshop, where he had Santos Hernández and Domingo Esteso as co-workers. In 1895, he moved to Barcelona and set up his own workshop. According to Domingo Prat, he was his promoter and that helped him to become well-known and appreciated in Argentina. He died in Barcelona on 31 October 1922. Personally, I give credence to the claim that García was a maestro of the calibre of Torres and Santos Hernández, although I never handled any of his guitars. But there is no doubt about the honor he gave the trade with the quality of his work, and the distinction he gave Barcelona as an excellent guitar-making area.

Francisco Simplicio: He was born in Barcelona in 1874. He started in woodwork as a cabinetmaker and managed to shine in this profession. He abandoned cabinet-making as a result of a labor strike, which brought about the closure of the workshop where he was first handyman. In 1919, Enrique García, who knew of Francisco's skills in woodwork, took him on as his assistant. He quickly rose to the position of first handyman, standing in for his master when he was on sick leave. In 1922, he assumed full control of the Enrique Garcia's workshop, earning the best guitar craftsmanship distinction. He attended several international fairs and won big prizes in 1929. He died in Barcelona in 1932. I have had the satisfaction of handling several guitars made by this estimable colleague. His handiwork was excellent, and the presentation and sound quality of his guitars were just perfect; all of which makes his guitar a luthier's instrument, constructed by an exemplary maestro. He was succeeded by his son.

Miguel Suplicio: I personally know his guitars. In 1933, the *Diario de Barcelona* newspaper published an article on this luthier. As of today, this old company forms part of the luthier guitar-making fraternity prior to the wars (1936–1945)

Don Ignacio Fleta: Since the end of the 1950s, was the most prestigious luthier guitar maker in Barcelona. A native of Huesca, he was born on 21 July 1897 and died in Barcelona in 1977. A cabinetmaker's son, he learned the noble work of woodcraft from his father. Like several professionals in this trade, his musical vocation led him to learn to play the banduria and the guitar, hence his curiosity for making musical instruments. He moved to Barcelona in his youth and trained as an apprentice under a French luthier. In 1927, he set up his own workshop, constructing violoncellos and, later on, violins and guitars. In 1955, Ignacio showed one of his guitars to the illustrious Andrés Segovia. The maestro was so impressed with it that he played it in a number of concerts all over the world, alternating it with his other guitar from Madrid. From the time Andrés Segovia used his guitar, Ignacio dedicated himself exclusively, together with his sons, to making concert guitars.

In the purest tradition of the old school, Ignacio and his sons, Francisco and Gabriel, rarely produced more than a couple dozen guitars a year, which indicates their total commitment to the scrupulous handcraft method. Each and every one of their guitars becomes nothing less than an unrepeatable instrument; in short, a work of art.

Ignacio's sons carry on his work, creating *la guitarra Fleta*. There is no doubt that Ignacio Fleta was its foremost maestro.

Others in Guitar-Making in Barcelona Today

Juan Estruch (Barcelona).

J. Ferré (Villafranca del Penedes).

José Masó (Barcelona).

Guitarras Mayoral (Barcelona).

Hermanos Yagüe (Barcelona).

Ramón Serra (Barcelona).

Diego Cortés (Pineda del Mar, Barcelona).

Antonio Sabate (Sant Cugat del Valles, Barcelona).

In Seville

Alberto Pantoja

Francisco Barba

Andrés Domínguez

Luis Puch

In Córdoba

Miguel Rodríguez Senior: A craftsman of the old school, and a descendant and disciple of the Madrid guitar luthier school. I had the honor of meeting him in Madrid in the early 1950s, when he came to deliver the guitar he had made for Mario Cubas, the famous collector; he gave me his business card, which I still have. His guitars were very popular in the hands of the Romero family, who were marketing them when I arrived in Los Angeles. He is succeeded by his son, who has maintained his school.

Manuel Reyes: An intuitive guitar maker, as he himself proclaims. He visited Marcelo in 1958. I cannot say he learned from Barbero, because this master virtually did not teach anyone. In all likelihood, Barbero must have given him some advice and shown him some of his constructions, as he did with other guitar makers of today. I am certain of what I am saying because I knew Reyes in those days—I was there. The perfection of his guitars makes them highly prized in flamenco circles.

Other guitar makers from Córdoba:

Aguilera Cañete (Córdoba).

Graciano Pérez (Córdoba).

Juan Montero (Córdoba).

Other Luthier Guitar Makers in Other Parts of the Country

Gerundino Fernández (Almería).

Geronino Peña (Jaén).

José Luis Marín (Málaga).

José Rodríguez Peña (Andújar, Jaén).

José Ruiz (Marmolejo, Jaén).

Luis Miguel Maldonado (Málaga).

Pedro Maldonado (Torremolinos, Málaga).

Vicente Carillo (Casasimarro, Cuenca).

Valeriano Bernal (Algodonales, Cádiz).

Tomás Leal (Cuenca).

Our Store in Madrid on Horaleza Street

Norman Rodriguez in his Workshop in the Back of the Shop

London: Mairants Music Centre

Mr. and Mrs. Drumm, Mr. and Mrs. Ivor Mairants, and Manuel Rodriguez Jr.

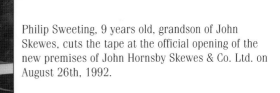

Philip Sweeting, 9 years old, grandson of John Skewes, cuts the tape at the official opening of the new premises of John Hornsby Skewes & Co. Ltd. on August 26th, 1992.

Mr. John W. Duarte and myself.

My classical guitar, Madrid 1957.

Memorable Guitar Personalities

This century has known a great number of music pedagogues who have enriched our guitar raising knowledge to its highest expression. I had the honor of meeting and dealing with, and in some cases make a guitar for them, after the ones I made in my youth in Spain.

Professor Theodore Norman (UCLA. 1965–97): Through his friendship I came to know many people who were enamoured of our guitar. In particular, our intimate friend and brother, Mr. Arthur E. Macbeth, an adviser of incomparable sincerity. His work as a guitar teacher, composer and music transcriber for the guitar left us a right heritage. However his greatest heritage of all was his tremendous personality, culture and humanity, which my family and I were privileged to enjoy. Thank you Ted, your memory will live on forever in the Rodriguez family.

Mr. José Barroso: First violoncellist and an eminent guitar teacher.

Vicente Gómez: My fellow compatriot, dear friend, and teacher of teachers.

Manuel Sanguesa.

Mr. Mariano Córdoba: Thanks to his flamenco dexterity, did so much for Spain in San Francisco.

Andrés Batista: The great guitarist and pedagogue.

Frederick Noad: The eminent and great diffusor.

Mr. John Gavall and **Mr. Thomas F. Heck.**

Mr. Ronald C. Purcell.

Mr. Aaron Shearer.

Mr. Graham Wade.

Mr. Wilfred Appleby: My acknowledgement to him and his magazine *The Guitar News*, which has done so much for the guitar.

Mr. John W. Duarte: I owe a special gratitude to him.

Barry Mason: The eminent and future guitarist.

Santiago Nacascues: My compatriot who makes our guitar in Munich.

Emilio Pugol: The eminent and excellent pedagogue and composer.

Mr. David Russell: Today's talent who, not only through his concerts, but thanks to his classes, creates a future enthusiasm for our guitar.

Christer Hellguest & **Stepan Lofvenius:** My friends in Sweden, who create enthusiasm for our guitar with their classes.

Mr. José Tomás: His teachings are extraordinarily paving the way for our guitar for future generations.

The **Valdés Blain brothers:** In New York, who for the numerous years have provided excellent teaching.

It is absolutely impossible to name all those experts of our guitar who are making it known and creating enthusiasm all over the world. I ask all those not mentioned here to forgive me.

However, as a luthier who earns his living from making guitars, I cannot end this section without expressing my gratitude to our great diffuser, **Mr. Maurice Summerfield**, for his book *The Classic Guitar,* and for his monthly magazine of the same name, as well as to his collaborators and collegues, **Mr. Colin Cooper** and **Mr. Christ Kilvington**.

And signing off to all the great guitarists who consider themselves "second to none."

To the **Romero Family**, who since their arrival to the USA, in the same year as my wife and myself, have been giving classes and concerts and making good fortune by constantly spreading the knowledge of our guitar.

The future will honor us all

The Rodriguezes visiting Mr. Joaquin Rodrigo
on his 97th birthday.

Maurice J. Summerfield, guitarist and a promulgator of our guitars around the world.

Theodore Norman (1912–1997)

Laurindo Almeida (1917-1995)

Andrés Segovia: I had the honor of dealing with him in the early years of the '50s, I made the acquaintance of Mr. Andrés Segovia, who was introduced to me by José Ramírez III when I was his assistant.

Mr. Andrés Segovia came to Madrid, his friend Dr. Rubio, who was also José Ramírez's friend, wanted to show him one of the José Ramírez personal guitars.

Through Dr. Rubio, Andrés Segovia came to the Ateneo in Madrid to try out this guitar on the stage and listen to it from the orchestra stalls. For the audition, Ramírez brought along the eminent concert guitarist, Mr. Narcisco Yepes, who, even in those days, enjoyed a certain prestige.

If memory serves me right, I think on that occasion Yepes was introduced to Master Segovia.

Years later, in 1958, when I was well-established, I attended the premier of the "Un Gentil Honbre" concert by Rodrígo, which the master performed at the Teatro Monumental de Madrid.

In 1959, I moved to Los Angeles; and in all those years that I lived there, I attended all Segovia's concerts in that city's two auditoriums: the University of Los Angeles and the one downtown.

I almost invariably entered the backstage to greet him, and on one occasion, I visited him in his hotel.

In Los Angeles, his concerts were usually around the beginning of the year. At about this time, in 1970, I presented him, during a visit I paid him at his hotel, a guitar. He played the guitar for a while without uttering a word, scrutinizing it here and there. He finally broke the silence and said to me, "I like your guitar, but my time to try it is really short; why don't you send it to me in Madrid so I can take all the necessary time to try it and study it."

"I will be happy to do that," I told him. That summer, through a friend who was coming to Madrid, I sent the guitar to my sisters to deliver it to Andrés Segovia's residence on Concha Espina Street.

My sisters did so, and came out feeling really pleased with the way the master had received them in his residence.

In November of that same year, the master wrote me a letter from Munich. On my return to Madrid, and several years after setting up my new workshop, I gave him a call and booked an appointment to visit him at his house. I visited him several times afterwards, and I was always well and warmly received.

I sincerely think that he quite liked the guitar I gave him, although he asked me to bring a few guitars for him to choose from. This I promised to do, but alas I was not able to deliver on that promise.

In those years, I was overwhelmed by my orders and it was difficult for me to present him with even three guitars at any given time. Time was running out, and the master passed away; my promise remained unfulfilled. And I never heard any more about the guitar I gave him, whose serial number is Los Angeles 1970 No. 315. With the passage of time, this guitar has fallen into oblivion.

In my luthier professional life, just as my colleagues do, I harbor the hope that a great artist will play my instrument. Not to mention that it really was a great honor that the master performed his concerts with a guitar made by me. The funny thing is that the one who had this honor was unable to make the most of it.

As far as I know, the master only played two handcrafted guitars, made personally by the luthiers themselves. One was constructed by the German Hauser, and the other by Ignacio Fleta.

The guitar by Manuel Ramírez was constructed by Santos Hernández, and those by José Ramírez were actually made by his workers. Anyway, whatever guitar that Andrés Segovia played at his concerts sounded marvellous and pleasantly delighted his world audience.

I am eternally grateful to have had the honor and delight of his consideration of my person and my work. I delighted in personally listening to him, and hearing him play my guitar. I thank him for generating appreciation and enthusiasm for our guitars all over the world. We owe him the highest esteem for his recognition of our guitar as a musical instrument of unique qualities.

Hotel Vier Jahreszeiten - Restaurant Walterspiel

Absender ist nicht das Hotel

8 MÜNCHEN 1º Nov. 1970
Maximilianstraße 17
Postamt 1 — Postschließfach 429

Sr. D. Manuel Rodriguez.

Estimado amigo: Perdone V. mi largo silencio. Se me han acumulado tantos viajes y conciertos que desaparecieron de mi memoria muchas cartas importantes que debía haber escrito —entre ellas la de V.

Su guitarra me gustó mucho. Está muy bien construida, muy cuidados los detalles y de mayor volumen sonoro que ninguna de las que he probado, hechas por V., hasta ahora. Espero volver a casa en Diciembre y probarla más detenidamente.

Fernruf: 22 88 21 — Fernschreiber: 05/23 859 — Telegramme: Walterspiel — Postscheck: München 57 47

Y entonces le daré una opinión más completa y mejor fundada. Su hermana de V. y su cuñado me la trajeron a casa, cuando yo estaba en plena organización de mi tournée por Europa. Sus parientes son muy simpáticos y me alegré de conocerlos. Vuelvo a pedirle perdón por la tardanza de estas líneas. Le agradezco mucho su envío y le exhorto a que siga V. trabajando con entusiasmo.

Suyo afmo

148

Chapter 5

The Guitar in Europe

*Vino, sentimiento, guitarra y poesía
hacen los cantares de la patria mía.
Cantaré
Quien dice cantares dice Andalucía.
A la sombra fresca de la vieja parra,
un mozo moreno rasguea la guitarra.
Cantares.
Algo que acaricia y algo que desgarra.
La prima que canta y el bordón que llora.
Y el tiempo callado se va hora tras hora. Cantares.
Son dejos fatales de la raza mora.
No importa la vida, que ya está perdida,
y después de todo, ¿qué es esto, la vida, la vida?
Cantares.
Cantando la pena, la pena se olvida.
Madre, pena, suerte, pena, madre, muerte,
ojos negros, negros y negra suerte.
Cantares.
En ellos el alma del alma se vierte.
Cantares.
Cantares de la patria mía,
quien dice cantares dice Andalucía.
Cantares.
No tiene más notas la guitarra mía*

CANTARES, by *MANUEL MACHADO*

5.1. Linguistic Origin of the Guitar; The Guitar in Europe; Personalities and Credentials.

Tar (Persian)
Kithara (Greek)
Qithara (Arabic)
Chitarra (Italian)
Quitarra (Ancient Spanish)

The Guitar in Germany; Its Beginnings and Development

In 1788, the Grand Duchess of Saxe-Weimar, Anna Amalia, a composer and a patron of the arts, introduced into her court an instrument from Italy which, in those days, was called *guitarra española* (the Spanish guitar).

The guitar was widely played and highly valued by the nobles of the Court. Subsequently, it became popular as a folklore instrument. The year 1788 appears to be crucial for the growth of the Spanish guitar in Germany.

The Spanish Guitar in Italy

In Spain, the Spanish guitar was introduced much earlier than in Germany. In all likelihood, the Kingdom of Naples introduced it into the Italian society during the period stretching from 1504 to 1647, when the first princes of the Habsburg family controlled the Kingdom of the Two Sicilies. (Spaniards then owned the Duchy of Milan, which included Pavia, where Francesco Corbetta was born.)

Musical Notation for the Six-Stringed Guitar

The first universally known method was by Francis Moretti from Naples, as found in his *Principles for Playing the Six Stringed Guitar*. Other methods were: *La tablatura y la medida notación* (by Antonio Abreu) and *Escuela para tocar con perfección la guitarra de 5 y 6 órdenes* (Salamanca 1799). Another was *Fernandière's Arte de tocar la guitarra española por música* (Madrid 1799), an attempt for the 6- and 11-stringed guitar. This method was born during a time of splendor in Spain, in Goya's time, before the invasion and the War of Independence. The book paved the way for the possibility of playing any piece on the guitar in accompaniment of any other instrument and within an orchestra. Before then, the reading for the interpretation of a composition for the guitar was based on figures and chords.

Personalities

Andrés Segovia was the foremost exponent, a romantic, and essentially the spiritual leader of our guitar. In a speech delivered when he was awarded a doctorate degree by the University of Florida (USA), he had these resounding words to say: "This is a legend of beauty as extraordinary as truth itself. Orpheus, the god, was said to be pursuing a beautiful nymph; when he eventually managed to get her to come into his arms, she invoked the name of her divine father, who instantly converted her into a precious tree. It was a laurel tree. Orpheus, enamoured, constructed a guitar with this tree. The curves in the guitar thrilled him so much because of the likeness to the feminine body of his nymph."

What is more, apart from its curve, the spirit of the guitar is very feminine indeed.

Despite the fact that the guitar is an uncertain instrument, it is, by the same token, the sweetest, the warmest, and the most delicate instrument that has ever existed. With its melancholic sounds it elevates the soul to exquisite heights of untold reverences. Allow me to say with pride that our guitar is profoundly Spanish and universal in its development. The Spaniard is rich in his/her emotions and individualistic. It is like his/her own society and, by analogy, the guitar adopts a rich polyphony, and with its range of colorful melodies, plays music as though it were an entire orchestra.

The Handicrafts Manual of Madrid

The description of the Royal Court and the Villa of Madrid by Don Ramón de Mesoneros Romanos, 1831 and 1844 goes as follows: "According to the present statutes, which I have in front of me, I can ascertain that in Madrid, there are the following factories and workshops: 200 carpenters, 22 cabinet-makers, 20 coach builders, 32 saddle makers, 15 guitar makers, 70 spearhead makers, etc. Up to 81 trades of all shades and kinds."

He continues: "In spite of all this, it seems that the industry in Madrid cannot be any more limited, seeing that it really does nothing other than meet and provide for the daily needs of the community.

"Guitar construction remains in a passive state under the oppressive weight of the regulations governing the trade. The guitar has experienced singular improvements in form and construction and, as a result, now has a stronger tone. More and more, it is being recommended as an instrument characteristic of Madrid and our nation. Nevertheless, we believe that its production has dropped from the throne to which it was once elevated by such famous people as Muñoa and the like."

The Guitar Battene

The guitar battene is quite different from the normal guitar. The back is curved and the proportion of the body to the neck is different. The body is exceptionally long. The fingerboard ends where the soundboard begins. The soundhole is a fine piece of fretwork, slightly sunken into the soundboard. It has nine frets of gut tied to the neck.

This guitar with five double strings has ten pegs. The strings pass over the bridge and are tied in pairs to five nails in the end block.

Thomas T. Heck, 1971: The Birth of the Classic Guitar

Thomas Heck talks about guitar strings and their possibilities in the function of the left hand. The guitar should never have adopted a string scale longer than 60 cm. Dr. Heck deplores the fact that in a super-long string scale, it is nearly impossible to manage a stretch to the 5th fret without an extreme effort and I could not agree with him more. Remember that the music of Giuliani and Sor, in addition to many others of that period, was composed for a string scale of not more than 63 cm.

I have constructed guitars with a 63.5-cm string scale. Surely a guitar of this dimension is a delight for interpreting music in any epoch, as long as the auditorium is small. The sound is sweet and sonorous and exquisitely balanced, and it makes an ideal instrument for others. Never stretch the sound, for with this string scale, you cannot force the sound to achieve more volume. This, simply, is the reason why luthiers, in reaction to the guitarist's demand for more volume, abandoned the 63.5-cm scale.

But do not make the mistake of thinking that the guitar is popular only today. According to Frederic Grunfeld, who was quoting the musicologist D. C. Burney of England at the end of the 18th century, "the fierce competition between guitar makers and those of the harpsichord was inevitable." There was "a boom so great" that it nearly ruined harpsichord and spinet makers.

In Spain at the beginning of 17th century, Diego de Torres Villaroel (1693–1770) used to say that here everyone knew how to dance and play the guitar a little. "In present-day Madrid there are 4,000 musicians—more than in the days of King Felipe III." It used to be said that, during that period, playing the guitar among the student population of the University of Salamanca was a remarkable expression of cultural and artistic capabilities.

Plucking-and-Plectrum Instruments; Their Orchestra, Serenader Troupes, Trios, Quartets, and Soloists

In my experience as a guitar maker, it was customary to learn the trade by starting out as an apprentice—generally a young boy aged 14, but not younger, because it was unlawful. When he began to get to know the tools and the woods, this young apprentice would take his first luthier steps, making bandurias and lutes—naturally, after having helped his masters construct and finish different pieces of these instruments. It was with these bandurias, bandurrines, lutes, tenors, baritones, and basses, together with guitars and bass guitars, that the groups of serenaders, quartets, and trios were formed. More often than not, some soloists of the musical groups outshone the others. In general, they were amateur and self-taught players of a plucking-and-plectrum instrument.

Ukrainian Bandura
Spanish Banduria by A. Viudes (1890)

If one more time we fold the map of Europe into two, on the one end, as I said before, would be Russia. Well, the word "bandura" appears in Ukraine, Mongolia, and Tartary. Descended from the Ukrainian korza, the bandura appeared in Spain at the beginning of 12th century, at the Tartar border of the Crimea. Popular in Poland, it first had 8 to 13 strings, and subsequently, 18 to 20; just as the 17th-century lute, the so-called "angelic," differed from the 16th-century lute by having 11 strings. (There were others, such as the alto, tenor, and bass lute, with various string thickness and scales.)

Like the lutes and other instruments of the Middle Ages, the korza-bandurias, Russo-Ukrainian, were fanciful in shape and construction, and in most cases, were made by the musician himself; which is why these instruments have diverse stringing methods, featuring strings of various thicknesses and scales.

With these instruments, the ordinary people enjoyed their bonanzas, festivities, ceremonies, and family gatherings. They were used in their folk dances, songs, choirs, and religious expressions. Today, they are admired for their richness and musical variation, and their capacity to produce wonders in the chants and dances of the folk heritage.

The Ukrainian banduria, similar to our calvete, is closer to the typical Portuguese guitar than to the more traditional spanish banduria in the shape of a pear. The strings are tied in the headstock, more or less as in the violin, and it has a similar scroll. The bridge is a strip of wood adjusted to the string scale, and it holds the strings that are finally tied at the tailpiece, in the lower part of the instrument; which in professional parlance is called the "end block," where the sides join together.

As a point of interest, I would like to relate what Mr. L. Haydamaka said: "Among the amazing musicians of this Ukrainian banduria, the one that outclassed them all was Professor H. Khotkevich, who was a highly talented composer. Also, he distinguished himself as a performer of great folklore purity, as well as being a singer and a banduria soloist. Between 1925 and 1936, he was giving banduria classes at the Conservatory of Kharkov, setting cathedra and forming disciples who, in time, became outstanding players of this instrument. In 1936, he was arrested, and that was the last we heard about him."

The instruments that guitar luthiers of my generation and school constructed in our initial stages are the so-called "plucking-and-plectrum" instruments: alto bandurríns, bandurias, baritone lutes, tenor lutes, flat mandolins, and guitars. These were the instruments with which groups of serenaders and plucking-and-plectrum string orchestras were formed. Well, unquestionably, these did not originate in those historical instruments used by the biblical Mediterranean countries in their music and folklore. Even so, we must not forget that in Asia, too, plucking-and-plectrum stringed instruments were used. A country on the shores of the Black Sea, in the Ukrainian steppe, developed nomad folklore of diverse dialects that used instruments such as these to accompany their songs and dances.

As in the case of the lute in Central Europe, these men from Ukraine and Russia earned their living by constructing these typical instruments of the steppe. A perfect example is the torban, which, like the baroque lute, had an infinity of strings. And, like the European lutes, they were pear-shaped. One of these torbans, constructed in the 19th century, had practically the same features as the baroque lute as created by any Austrian or Italian luthier. Like their baroque counterparts, these had two set of worm gears where the bass strings were exposed over an ebony bridge that went from one side of the soundboard to the other, holding 30 strings. fourteen of these strings were held by a worm gear on the treble side and inserted into the bridge loop. Another twelve went from the bridge to the gear, over the gut frets, along the fingerboard. The four bass strings were in the open, with a separate third gear. The length of the torban was 118 cm, and the width of the soundboard measured 37 cm. As we will see, this instrument is a cousin of the numerous baroque instruments of the same family

What is not really clear in all this is whether the torban, having the same features as our banduria, was created before or after that of the shape as we know it. What seems to be confirmed is that it was the Arabs who, through Spain during the century of conquest, introduced these instruments in their various string forms and tuning into Western Europe. In the East, they were introduced through China, Turkey, and India; also in different kinds.

The Spanish lute is mentioned by the Archpriest of Hita and the Archpriest of Talavera in their writings of 1250. These lutes seem to have been similar to those inherited from the Arabs, since that was the instrument of the troubadours of the Spanish Mediterranean coast.

The banduria was described by J. Bermudo in 1555 as a "superb instrument." At first these instruments, which were smaller than the lute, had a body in the shape of an animal shell or skin. Over the centuries, as in the case of the lute, the body came to be made with wood and the soundhole had a fretwork rosette. It was in 1600 when frets were first used.

In Spain, with the passage of time, these instruments were used by soloists and music groups. Traditionally, young students, music groups in every university, troubadours, and poets sang to youth and their loved ones while playing these instruments.

These groups of banduria, lute, and guitar players ("rondallas") formed part of the life in the cities, towns, and villages, enlivening religious moments, family fiestas, baptisms, and marriage ceremonies.

In Aragón, typically, it was *de rigueur* to use them to play the vibrant jotas. In Andalusia, they are a must in the zambras (Gypsy festivities) and the sevillanas dance. In actual fact, in every region, in their own particular way, different styles of jota are sung and danced to with the accompaniment of the guitar, banduria, and lute.

Its Construction

The most ancient that I have ever seen, whether banduria or lute, had six double strings, or, if you prefer, twelve strings, made of gut and silk attached to wooden pegs. In modern times, they come with mechanical gears and steel strings.

Once again in this book I would take the liberty to insert a beautifully written letter, from the honorable Manuel de Falla to the distinguished Emilio Pujol:

To Emilio Pujol, most respected friend:

Would that I were a Llobet or a Segovia so that I could speak fittingly about your Guitar Method, and therefore return the affectionate kindness with which you have honored me by asking me to give a few words of introduction. But what could I add to the excellent practical and theoretical teachings that we all owe you? If there is anything that I can say it will be to pay homage to this instrument, which has always occupied a favourite place in all the Hispanic households where it has paid a resounding visit, and whose history is so often interwoven into our own history as well as into the very history of European music in general.

An admirable instrument, as sober as it is rich, which either roughly or sweetly takes possession of the spirit, and which, with its walk through time, has accumulated the essential values of the former noble instruments from which it has received so much heritage without losing its own character, which it owes to the people on account of its origin.

How can I not affirm that, of all the stringed instruments with a neck, the guitar is the richest and the most complete because of its harmonic and polyphonic properties? But even if all this were not enough to illuminate its significance, the history of music has shown us its magnificent influence, as a transmitter of the essential Hispanic sound, throughout the great musical art sector of Europe. With what emotions we discover its brilliant reflections in Domenico Scarlatti, in Glinka, and in Debussy and Ravel! And were we to look then into our own music, which, secularly, owes so much to its influence, it would suffice to cite the recent example of the splendid Iberia that Isaac Albéniz has left us.

But let us come back to the work that you have offered us. Since the distant times of Aguado, we have been lacking a complete Method that could pass on the technical progress initiated by Tárrega. You, with yours, have achieved this goal excellently, together with your personal contribution, thereby benefiting not only the performer but also the composer with a sharp sensibility, who will find in your Method reasons to further enhance his sensibility, as he discovers fresh instrumental possibilities.

My heartfelt congratulations and warmest greetings to you.

With all my admiration and love, your friend,

MANUEL DE FALLA
Granada. December 1933

OPINIONS:

Thomas T. Heck

Thomas Heck asks if the development of guitar in the 17th and 18th centuries was different from its development in Italy and Austria in the same period. He answers himself by saying that the guitar was not a folk instrument, in that Spanish and Italian concert guitarists wrote very respectable and refined music for this instrument. It remained as the only instrument in the higher spheres of the noble class in the various European royal courts, from the 17th to the 19th centuries, competing with the incipient piano and nearly causing the disappearance of the baroque lute.

Features Required of the Guitar by Dionisio Aguado

Considering that everyone thinks of their guitar as the best, I will dare to make a description of a guitar that I possess, constructed by Juan Muñoa and perhaps the best instrument ever made by this guitar maker.

Referring to Muñoa's method, Dionisio Aguado had this to say to guitarists in 1825: "This method is sold in the Muñoa guitar workshop, at Angosta de Majaderitos Street (Madrid). For more than 270 years the guitar (formerly vihuela) has been recognized as an instrument of harmony." (*Pisador: Libro de cifra para tener vihuela*, Salamanca, 1552.)

The point is this: with a guitar that has a bad sound, a bad fretting method, disproportionately sized strings that are hard, badly shaped and constructed, and is old and dull, how can any musician excel, however skillful he might be? His guitar needs a good sound, the right proportions, a short neck and an accurate division of the 12 frets (up to just about the point where the sides of the soundboard should converge).

For many aficionados, Muñoa's disappearance was a sad event. However, some work undertaken by his nephew and disciple, Antonio Muñoa, have raised hopes that his skill will be continued.

Dionisio Aguado said in his new method for the guitar (3rd edition, Madrid, Benito Campo, 1849): "And all these works are sold only at Benito Campo's guitar workshop, at 16 Majaderitos Street, Madrid." Benito Campo was the man who took control of Muñoa´s guitar workshop on Majaderitos Street following the disappearance of Manuel, Juan, and Antonio Muñoa.

Rosette design by my son Norman, our company's official rosette designer.

Notes on the Guitar That You Enjoy

The Mosaic and Ornamentation on the Soundhole

In the 17th century, our guitars began to be decorated with mosaic around the soundhole; but previously, mother-of-pearl and marquetry, in small amounts, had been used on the soundboard, although they were not engraved.

An engraved filigree cast on wood and inlaid on the circumference of the soundhole (the so-called guitar batene) distinguished the ancient lutes from guitars. The luthier then devised a way of inlaying the veneer, mosaic, and mother-of-pearl, casting them on the wood around the soundhole so that he could introduce the ornamentation he wanted.

Certainly, the guitar that you play and enjoy is decorated with a beautiful mosaic, which you cannot fail to notice.

Regarding the mosaic and the rosette of the guitar, I can tell you that all the lines and points are veneer in its natural color, white, and the rest is dyed. The construction of the mosaic is extremely laborious and takes an awful lot of time. The veneer usually has a minimum of 4/10 or 6/10 mm thickness.

On the market, you can only get the 4/10 white veneer; the other colors, black, red, green, and yellow, come in 6/10–10/10 thickness. But the beautiful and delicate-looking mosaic has an optimum point of 3/10. The whole veneer must be reduced to 3/10 thickness, and there has yet to be a machine invented to aid the maker of handcrafted guitars. He has to reduce them by hand with the aid of a wood scraper. The veneer usually comes 2 cm wide and 80 cm long, and is reduced to the desired thickness.

My intention here is not to show you how difficult it is to make the mosaic, the plume, and the veneer that adorn your guitar. What I do want to do is draw your attention to the adornment on your guitar so that you appreciate it. Page 157 features one of the rosette designs that my son Norman, the official rosette designer of our company, created for one of our guitars. A luthier worthy of the name, he takes a lot of pride in creating, designing, and constructing a series of mosaics that, with a variant of herringbone purfling and veneer, adorn the guitars that he constructs throughout his professional life.

The satisfaction felt by luthiers from the Madrid school for the reputation of their rosettes and mosaics—for their variety, beautiful design, purity, and precision of construction—need scarcely be mentioned.

I have personally constructed the mosaics of the guitars that I have signed. Not many years ago, my sons and I became guitar manufacturers. We design the guitars, and we have them reproduced. It is humanly impossible to make the guitar rosette by hand when we construct several thousands of instruments per annum, but you can be sure that we are satisfied with our mosaics. The four luthiers of the Rodríguez family design a variety of delicate and fine rosettes of good quality and beauty. And we make them at any cost. Personally, I, Manuel Rodríguez Senior, can hardly resist creating various versions of my mosaics and plumes so that each and every one of the guitars made by my hands will be different from all the others made by me throughout my professional life.

The Fingerboard on the Soundboard up to the Soundhole

There is controversy as to which guitar luthier introduced this advance, but until otherwise proved, the first must have been Manuel Muñoa (1779–1815).

According to the *La Guitarra Española*, this guitar appears to be have been signed by this guitar maker and dated in 1804, and had a fingerboard extending to the soundhole; although this guitar by Muñoa must have been constructed with the fingerboard ending on the soundboard and subsequently prolonged. What I am sure about is that it must have been reconstructed by Muñoa himself.

There is evidence to the effect that this guitar maker was chosen by

Dionisio Aguado, the great pedagogue, guitarist, and harbinger of our guitar, who had brilliant ideas about improving our instrument. Muñoa must have gotten the idea from him to make the fingerboard reach the soundhole, in one piece and close to the soundboard and neck joint. There is no doubt that this greatly improved the sound of Muñoa's guitars. Regrettably, not many guitars from that epoch have survived to our day. As a proof of this, I would like to cite from the *Gallery of Guitars* the following guitar makers, who closed the neck and soundboard joint with the fingerboard:

Guitar no.12	Joan Matabosch. Barcelona, 1815
Guitar no. 3	Anónimo. Madrid 18...
Guitar no.14	A. Caro. Granada 18...3
Guitar no.15	Salvador Pau. Valencia, 1830
Guitar no.16	Manuel N. González. Madrid, 1833
Guitar no.17	Luis Reig. Valencia, 1845
Guitar no.18	Francisco Pages. Havana, 1835
Guitar no.19	Antonio Lorca. Málaga, 1847

So, as we can see, all the guitar makers named in the *La Guitarra Española* constructed guitars on which the fingerboard ends up at the soundhole.

Today, the guitar is produced all around the globe, thanks to the initiative and common sense with which guitar makers of bygone days managed to perfect its construction system. They created the current guitar, the modern guitar of our days, which we, luthier guitar makers the world over, have observed, learned from and constructed.

No matter how hard we attempt to change it or rely on physicists, mathematicians, and doctors of higher learning to improve upon it, it is similar to that of past guitar maestros: a copy of the same thing, with variations on the theme.

I beg to differ with the authors of the wonderful book *Guitars from the Renaissance to Rock*, Tom Evans and Mary Anne Evans; and by the same token prove to them that they are wrong in affirming (page 42) that the first guitar luthier to prolong the fingerboard to the soundhole was the German George Staufer, who, according these famous writers, was granted a licence together with Joseph Estel in 1822. I imagine it might have been a patent licence or a professional one from the guild. It should be recalled that my compatriot and Madrilenian colleague was born in 1779 and died in 1815, and that the above-mentioned licence was granted seven good years after Muñoa's death. Furthermore, other Spanish guitar makers were already prolonging the fingerboard to the soundhole, as can be observed on the guitars in *La Guitarra Española*, to which I have made reference above, with names and dates.

Another guitar luthier of the Madrid school who was ahead of his time was Juan Moreno, on whose guitar, dated 1830, we observe the change to the modern system of fingerboard and soundhole joint, bracings under the soundboard, and bridge with inlaid bone saddle. Moreno, who died in 1836, greatly influenced on his colleagues Manuel Narciso González and Francisco González, as can be seen in the guitars they constructed respectively in 1833 and 1865. Juan Moreno also collaborated with Aguado. To lend weight and formality to my statements, I have cited three articles from the *Great Gallery of Guitars* (*Guitar Review* Nos. 30, 32, and 35), out of the nearly sixty guitars featured in the collection. I would like you, dear reader, to know that in these three issues of this reputable magazine you can find a series of beautifully and fantastically constructed guitars from all the countries of Europe. There is only one six-stringed guitar, maker unknown, constructed in the closing years of 19th century, which has the fingerboard up to the soundhole.

El canto del arpa es una alegría;
el canto del piano es un discurso,
el canto de la guitarra es un canto.
                              GERARDO DIEGO

5.2. My Credentials

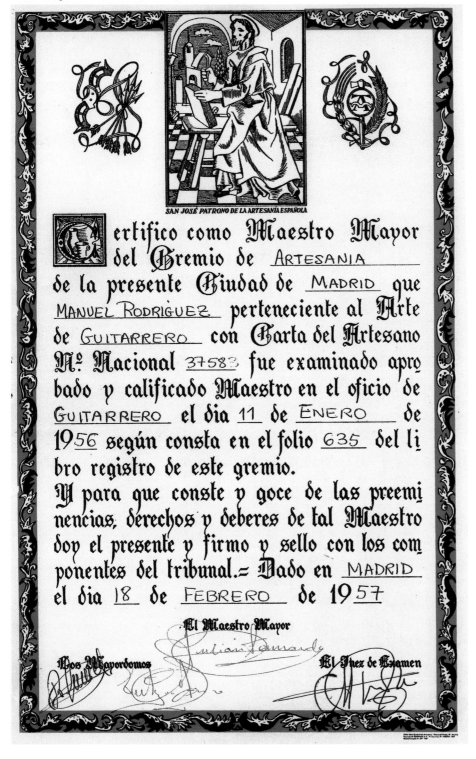

SAN JOSÉ PATRONO DE LA ARTESANÍA ESPAÑOLA

Certifico como Maestro Mayor del Gremio de ARTESANIA de la presente Ciudad de MADRID que MANUEL RODRIGUEZ perteneciente al Arte de GUITARRERO con Carta del Artesano Nº Nacional 37583 fue examinado aprobado y calificado Maestro en el oficio de GUITARRERO el dia 11 de ENERO de 1956 según consta en el folio 635 del libro registro de este gremio.

Y para que conste y goce de las preeminencias, derechos y deberes de tal Maestro doy el presente y firmo y sello con los componentes del tribunal. = Dado en MADRID el dia 18 de FEBRERO de 1957

El Maestro Mayor

Los Mayordomos   El Juez de Examen

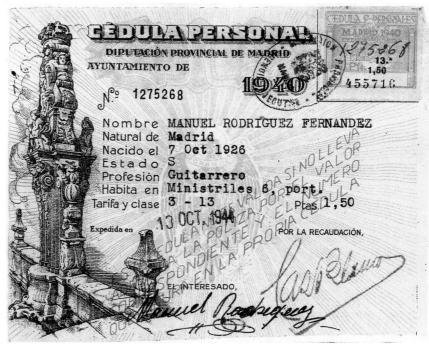

The Years and Labels of Our Guitars

1943–1950

1950–1957

1957–1959

Los Angeles 1959–1973

1973–1979

Year 1979: My label for my personally made guitar.

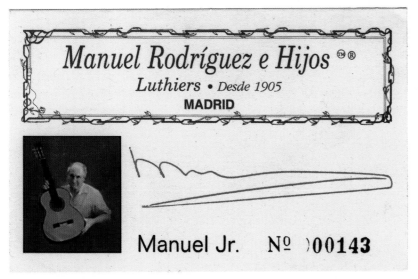

Actual Manuel Rodriguez Jr.

Actual Norman Rodriguez.

The labels of our guitars built in our shop in Exquivias.

Chapter 6

Music with World Leaders

*We have learned that we live in
a very small world. We work with
world leaders, giving them guitars
to communicate the message
that it is important to support
music for education and children.*

MANUEL RODRÍGUEZ, SR.

Continuing the Tradition

As is clear from the preceding pages, Manuel Rodríguez, Sr., and the Rodríguez family were and continue to be dedicated to spreading the beauty of classical guitar and the culture of Spain throughout the world. When Manuel Rodríguez, Sr., passed away on December 25, 2008, after a long illness, his family and company, led by Manuel Rodríguez, Jr., continued the tradition of outreach to heads of state through the company's Music with World Leaders program. Led ceremonially by King Juan Carlos I, the program makes Guitarras Manuel Rodríguez and Sons an essential stop for visiting government officials. There dignitaries are exposed to the rich history of the Spanish guitar, which dates from the 14th century, and the Rodríguez family's efforts at bringing arts education to children and facilitating improved relations worldwide through the gift of music.

An impressive number of world leaders has embraced the Rodríguez mission, as internationally recognized foundations and charities have

CEOE President Gerardo Ferrán

President of Estonia, Toomas Hendrik Ilves

Prime Minister of Tunisia D. Mohamed Ghannouchi

benefited from the donations of Rodríguez instruments under the sponsorship of the King of Spain, the Federation of Entrepreneurs, and the General Chamber of Commerce of Spain.

The list of recipients includes the president of Uruguay, Tabaré Vázquez; the president of China, Hu Jintao; the president of Estonia, Toomas Hendrik Ilves; the president of Rumania, Traian Băsescu; the president of Costa Rica, Óscar Arias; the president of Hungary, Mr Ferenc Gyurcsány; the president of Tunez, Mohamed Ghannouchi; and of course the king of Spain, Juan Carlos I.

Work with president Jimmy Carter

In 2007, former U.S. president Jimmy Carter, a longtime fan of classical guitar dating from his time spent with Andres Segovia during the virtuoso's performance at the White House, visited Guitarras Manuel Rodríguez and Sons near Toledo in Spain to sign labels for guitars destined for the

Director of Tourism and Handicrafts
Magdalena Valerio

Georgia (USA) governor Sonny Perdue

President of Costa Rica Oscar Arias

JIMMY CARTER

March 14, 2008

To Manuel Rodriguez

Rosalynn and I appreciate your donation of a handmade Manuel Rodriguez Flamenco guitar to our 2008 Winter Weekend auction in Port St. Lucie, Florida. The auction is the highlight of the weekend, and the proceeds from this year's event will support our efforts to wage peace, fight disease, and build hope around the world. Your generosity and friendship are greatly appreciated.

Sincerely,

Jimmy Carter

Mr. Manuel Rodriguez Sr.
Manuel Rodriguez and Sons, S. L.
C/. Hortaleza, 26
28004 Madrid
SPAIN

Carter Center Winter Auction. In 2008 the company partnered with the Guitar Center Music Foundation and the Carter Center to donate one guitar per year for auction by the Center. Money raised by the auctions has been designated for many of the Carter Center's worldwide humanitarian efforts, such as combating river blindness in Africa.

The Carter Center's annual Winter Weekend auction, held February 7, 2009, at Port St. Lucie, Florida., raised $817,590 to help support the work of the not-for-profit organization, which works to promote peace and health worldwide. The highest-bid item at the fundraiser was an original painting by Jimmy Carter, which sold for $100,000. One of the other most successful auctions was a handmade Manuel Rodríguez classical guitar, which sold for $65,000.

Manuel Rodríguez, Jr., shows President and Mrs. Jimmy Carter a recently finished instrument.

The connection between the Guitar Center Music Foundation and the Carter Center came about in September of 2007, when Eric Spitzer, a Guitar Center vice president, attended a tour of Guitarras Manuel Rodríguez and Sons' manufacturing facility in Madrid, Spain. The tour had been arranged for President Carter and his wife, former first lady Rosalynn Carter, by Manuel Rodríguez, Jr. John Martin, longtime friend of the Carters and U.S. editor of Guitart International, spearheaded the project and introduced the idea of donating musical instruments.

The Rodríguez Classical Guitar Company had arranged to donate one specially made guitar per year for eight years that would be signed by President Carter and then auctioned for charity through the Carter Center. During the tour the new relationship between Guitar Center and the Carter Center was formed. In celebrating the music-education and humanitarian efforts of the Carter Center-Guitar Center partnership, Eric Spitzer commented, "I'd like to add how much the Guitar Center Music

US Ambassador to Spain Eduardo Aguirre and family

President of the Community of Madrid, Esperanza Aguirre

Foundation and I appreciate the help of the Rodríguez family and Rodríguez Classical Guitars in facilitating this relationship."

Guitars for the World

Typical of the many warm relationships with heads of state developed by Guitarras Manuel Rodríguez and Sons were the 2009 presentations of handmade classical guitars to Panamanian president Martin Torrijos and Bolivian president Evo Morales. The guitar maker called the gifts a symbol of brotherhood between the two countries and "a fundamental element of the culture shared by [the countries] and Spain." The guitars were built from Madagascar rosewood, Canadian cedar, Honduras cedar, and ebony. All of these woods, in keeping with Rodríguez manufacturing traditions, were at least 30 years old and naturally dried.

The craftsmanship and beauty of Rodríguez guitars is well known. The instruments have been used and praised by artists ranging from Andres

President of Panama D. Martin Torrijos

Prince Radu of Rumania

Segovia, Regino Sáinz de la Maza, and Angel Romero to Eric Clapton, Sting, and many others. Noted composer Joaquín Rodrigo recognized in 1989 Manuel Rodríguez, Sr.'s "great achievements for the Spanish guitar." In his lifetime Manuel Rodríguez enjoyed the recognition and admiration he deserved and won many prizes and awards. A dream of Manuel's was

President of Hungary Ferenc Gyurcsany

to meet President Jimmy Carter. He not only achieved that personal triumph, but also built a legacy that will endure, thanks to the efforts of Manuel Rodríguez, Jr., and family. Their outreach to world leaders will continue to ensure the promotion and celebration of Spanish culture and guitar, and their generous donation of beautiful instruments for auction will provide many thousands of dollars in funds to benefit humanitarian efforts around the world for years to come.

President of Uruguay Tabaré Vázquen, with Gerardo Díaz Ferrán, president of the CEOE

Bibliography

1. *The Art & Times of the Guitar.* Frederic V. Grunfeld (Collier Books, New York, 1969)

2. *The Physics of Music.* Alexander Wood

3. *Musical Acoustic.* Charles A. Culver, PhD

4. *Manual de Madrid* (description of Madrid). Don Ramón de Mesoneros Romanos (1831)

5. *The Birth of the Classic Guitar and Its Cultivation in Vienna.* Thomas T. Heck (Yale Univ., Conn. 1971)

6. *Understanding Wood.* R. Bruce Hoadley

7. *The World of Musical Instruments.* Alan Kendall

8. *The Meaning & Magic of Music.* Peter Gammond

9. *Manual of Guitar Technology.* Frank Jahnel

10. *Guitar Review* Nos. 29, 30, 32, and 35

11. *Violin Making.* Ed Heron-Allen

12. *Diccionario de guitarras, guitarristas y guitarreros, danzas y cantos terminología.* Domingo Prat (Buenos Aires, 1934)

13. *Tárrega: Ensayo biográfico.* Emilio Pujol (Lisboa, 1960)

14. *Inventario de guitarreros granadinos.* (1875–1983). Eusebio Rioja (Granada, 1983)

15. *Geometry, Proportions & the Art of Lutherie.* Kevin Coates (Clarendon Press, Oxford 1985)

16. *Early Music* magazine. Oxford University Press, UK

17. *The Classical Guitar, Its Evolution, Players and Personalities Since 1800.* Maurice J. Summerfield (Ashley Mark Publishing Co., UK, 2002)

18. *Un siglo de la guitarra granadina.* Manuel Cano (1975)

19. *Guitars from the Renaissance to Rock.* Mary & Tom Evans (London, 1977)

20. *The Flamenco Guitar.* David George (1969)

21. *La guitarra española.* José Villar Rodríguez (Barcelona, 1985)

22. *El derecho de ser hombre.* (Unesco, 1973)

23. *En tono a la guitarra: soneto.* José Ramírez III (Madrid, 1993)

24. *Antonio Stradivari, His Life & Work (1664–1737).* Hill Brothers (Dover Publications Inc., New York, 1963)

25. *My Fifty Fretting Years.* Ivor Mairants (Ashley Mark Publishing Co., UK, 1980)

26. *Memorias del flamenco.* Félix Grande (Madrid, 1979)

27. *Los instrumentos de púa en España.* Juan José y Antonio Navarro (Madrid, 1993)

28. *Violin Varnish.* Joseph Michelman (Cincinnati, USA, 1946)

29. *The Art of Wood Finishing.* H. Behlen Bro Inc. (New York, 1957)

30. *Guitar News.* (Cheltenham, UK, 1960)

31. *Historia de la música.* José Forns (Madrid, 1948)

32. *Antología iberoamericana de la guitarra.* Luis F. Leal Pinar (Madrid, 1843)

33. *Escuela de la guitarra.* Dionisio Aguado (Madrid, 1849; Paris, 1820)

34. *Nuevo método para guitarra.* Dionisio Aguado (Madrid, 1843)

35. *Escenas matritenses.* Mesoneros Romanos (Madrid, 183?, 1835)

36. *La guitarra española.* Museo Municipal (Madrid, 1991–1992)

37. *Antonio de Torres, Guitar Maker—His Life and Work.* José L. Romanillos (Element Books Ltd, Shaftesbury, UK, 1987)

38. *Tuning and Temperament: A Historical Survey.* J. Murray Barbour (Da Capo Press, New York, 1972)

39. *Intervals, Scales and Temperaments.* L. L. S. Lloyd and Hugh Boyle (St Martins Press, 1963, UK)

40. *Musical Instruments & Illustrated History.* Alexander Buchner (UK)

41. *The Encyclopaedia of Wood: A Tree by Tree Guide to the World's Most Versatile Resource.* John Makepeace and Aidan Walker (Oxford, UK, 1989)

42. *Timber.* Ralph W. Andrews (Schiffer Publishing Ltd, Exton, Pennsylvania, USA, 1968)

GREETINGS

How can I voice my greetings to my friends
The multitude of friends, near and afar?
How send the great goodwill my heart extends
To all who love and work for the guitar?
I will examine atlas, maps and charts.
Revolve my globe and place my finger here
On Australia - where my journey starts -
Africa, Asia, westward 'round the sphere
Through many-nationed Europe and then on
To vast America, the Pacific Isles -
Then I will waft to you my benison
And grasp imagined hands from countless miles.
Upon my charts I'll write for all to see
On every region: "Here guitarists be!"

(From Life Colour *by Wilfrid M. Appleby)*

In memory of Wilfrid Appleby; I join him in sharing the words of
this poem and send greetings to all the guitarists of this planet.